Purple Mountains

America From a Motorcycle

by Notch Miyake

A Whirlaway Book
Whitehorse Press
North Conway, New Hampshire

Whitehorse Press books are also available at discounts in bulk quantity for sales and promotional use. For details about special sales or for a catalog of motorcycling books and videos, write to the publisher:

Whitehorse Press
P.O. Box 60
North Conway, New Hampshire 03860-0060
Phone: 603-356-6556 or 800-531-1133
E-mail: Orders@WhitehorsePress.com
Internet: www.WhitehorsePress.com

ISBN 1-884313-28-0

5   4   3   2

Printed in the United States of America

Since this book was written, two of the people in it have died. My Auntie Kiyota passed away quietly, ending the old age she despised. I wish she were still with us complaining. She was the last of my mother's generation, the oldest of three sisters. She felt it was somehow unfair that she had lived the longest.

My shipmate Bill died of a stroke as he was planning a cross-country trip with his new wife. He was happily anticipating coming to Rochester to see us again. I'll miss swapping sea stories with him.

This book is for Auntie and Bill and everyone else whose life has touched mine. Only a few of you are in the book, but all of you are in my heart. Mahalo.

Contents

Part 1   The East

1 Preparations· · · · · · · · · · · · · · 10
2 Setting Out · · · · · · · · · · · · · 20
3 The East Coast · · · · · · · · · · · 25
4 The Atlantic· · · · · · · · · · · · · 36
5 Southwesterly· · · · · · · · · · · · 39
6 The Mississippi Valley · · · · · · · · 54
7 The Delta · · · · · · · · · · · · · · 64

Part 2   The West

8 Houston· · · · · · · · · · · · · · · 70
9 Texas · · · · · · · · · · · · · · · 73
10 New Mexico · · · · · · · · · · · · 82
11 Halfway · · · · · · · · · · · · · · 91
12 Las Vegas · · · · · · · · · · '· · · 98
13 Death Valley· · · · · · · · · · · · 103
14 California · · · · · · · · · · · · · 107
15 The West Coast · · · · · · · · · · 115

Part 3   Alaska

16 Olympia· · · · · · · · · · · · · · 120
17 Tacoma · · · · · · · · · · · · · 127
18 Port Orchard· · · · · · · · · · · · 130
19 Headed North · · · · · · · · · · · 137
20 Canada · · · · · · · · · · · · · 142
21 The Alaska Highway · · · · · · · · 150

22 Yukon Territory · · · · · · · · · · · 156
23 Alaska · · · · · · · · · · · · · · · 162
24 Going Home · · · · · · · · · · · · · 165
25 Haines · · · · · · · · · · · · · · · 171
26 The Inside Passage · · · · · · · · · 181

Part 4   The Midwest

27 Canada II · · · · · · · · · · · · · 186
28 The Rockies · · · · · · · · · · · · 191
29 The Great Plains · · · · · · · · · · · 198
30 Rochester, Minnesota · · · · · · · · 203
31 Rochester, New York · · · · · · · · 212

Postscript

About the Author

Acknowledgements

I originally intended to tell my wife Margaret and our two children, Dylan and Tama, about my trip across America. The story grew from a brief personal essay into a book as I tried to understand my experience as more than a list of places I had seen.

Margaret, as always, unquestioningly supported the entire project. Rafe Martin, storyteller and author, pushed me to finish the manuscript and encouraged me to try to get it published.

Lisa Dionne, editor at Whitehorse Press, rescued the book from the rejection pile and championed it. More importantly, she forced me to do the difficult work of digging for the truth instead of hiding behind superficial descriptions and thoughtless humor.

I am grateful to these three people for helping me share this with you.

Part 1
The East

1

Preparations

A break in my life made the trip possible. I sold my business and found myself unemployed at a time when I was beginning to question a lot of things.

Small business is tough. Perpetual lawsuits by partners and employees. Suspicious bankers. IRS tax audits. OSHA inspections. Demanding customers. Vendors who start worrying about being paid the moment they sell you something. Employees who were never truly appreciated or paid enough.

I was waking up with an aching jaw from grinding my teeth all night. Drinking enough at parties to repent the next morning. Becoming more and more compulsive about smaller and smaller things. Every time I saw the ding in the otherwise perfect car door I would become enraged. And I felt so tired I had to mentally force myself to begin a task.

I often found myself pulling into a parking space at work and not recalling how I had gotten there. The seasons passed unnoticed except for momentary discomfort as I passed between the conditioned air of my office, car, and home.

The preoccupation got extreme. At a party one evening, a woman remarked as we were talking, "You're always thinking, aren't you?" And I was suddenly aware that my mind had grabbed some business problem and had been racing away with it.

I couldn't remember the last time I had read a book for pleasure. My reading was mostly a desperate struggle to keep up with the technology and the economy. *The Wall Street Journal.* Scientific journals and trade publications. The business section of the local paper. I never missed anything. Hey, business is competitive and information is the key to survival.

I spent a week of numbed idleness after selling the business, then I found myself back on the phone working my contacts. Having lunch. Visiting lawyers and brokers. I met with people with ideas and no money. I met with people who had money but no ideas. And always, the familiar scent of desperation. Does my business plan make sense? Can I survive another month? Do I have enough to cover payroll this week?

I saw people looking for the big score. Wary. Working the deal. Most business plans aren't worth the time it takes to read them. Bet on the people, not the idea. Be sure they are motivated. Get them to pledge their house and all their assets before giving them a cent.

Did I really want to get back into all this bullshit?

Was this the dreaded mid-life crisis? I didn't know. But I knew I needed a change so I decided to take some time off and do a few things I have wanted to do for so long I had forgotten when I started wanting them or why.

I wanted to take the toys that had sat in my garage for years and transform them into real traveling machines instead of steel and aluminum shrines in remembrance of past glories and unachieved dreams. I wanted to know if I could do it, not merely dream it. So, what the hell.

Preparing for the ride began in midwinter. At the time, I had two project bikes in the garage, a 1974 BMW R75/6 and a Ducati 750GT. Neither of these could be put together in time for a summer ride. And twenty-year old aluminum on the Alaska Highway didn't sound like such a good idea, especially European aluminum, and one of them Italian.

A call to a friend and both machines were sold in two weeks. I started shopping for a new bike. For me, motorcycles represent an antidote to the complexity of modern life, so the new machine had to be simple. That meant no more than two cylinders, air-cooling, and valves that could be adjusted without removing the camshaft. Unfortunately, most brand new motorcycles fitting this description are dirt bikes, glorified mopeds, or third world transportation solutions.

The only new, two-cylinder, air-cooled, touring motorcycles available today are made by Harley-Davidson, BMW, Ducati, and Moto Guzzi. The Ducatis and Moto Guzzis were eliminated because they were exotic, wonderfully impractical, and sexier than hell. I still lust for the Ducati. The new Harleys and BMWs were eliminated because they were too expensive. Many brand new cars are cheaper. My only option was to look for a used bike, an impractical route in Rochester, New York, in the middle of winter.

Back at the dealerships, reluctantly prepared to spend more money, two-and-a-half options emerged:

1. A Harley-Davidson Sportster fitted with a slightly larger gas tank (but still too small) and a seat that looked a bit more comfortable (but still painful).

2. A BMW R100GS that was way too tall but had a gigantic gas tank and a comfortable seat.

2.5 The half-option was a Honda Transalp, a dirt bike arrested partway through its evolution into a GS. It was cheap because it was leftover from several model years before.

Digging through the Swap Sheet one day, however, I found an ad for a new GS listed for $1,000 less than the lowest price I could get anywhere else. It was even cheaper than many used GSs advertised in the *BMW Owners News,* a magazine for BMW motorcycle nuts. I called and it was for real, but it was purple. Oh.

Undeterred in my search for a bargain, I drove out for a look. The color kind of grows on you. I actually liked it by the time I wrote my deposit check. Two weeks later, during a mild snowstorm, I went back with two friends to get the bike. We lifted it onto the truck, unloaded it at home using a snowbank as an impromptu ramp, wheeled it into the garage, and parked it to wait for spring.

There wasn't much more I needed to get together. Motorcycle travel forces you to carefully evaluate your needs. There just isn't much space on a bike. So I passed on the nifty water purification kit and the ten-in-one pocket survival tool. I kept reminding myself that if I left out any essentials, I could always go to a store.

The campstoves and cooking sets were fascinating, but I decided instead to rely entirely on local restaurants. As well as eliminating a lot of stuff, I thought this would put me in closer contact with the people who lived in the places I would be going.

I got a tent from L.L. Bean. It was not the smallest nor the lightest dome tent they offered, but it was the cheapest. I cut a sheet of plastic from the hardware store into a ground cloth for the tent.

I bought a 3/4-length Thermarest sleeping pad. These things are surprisingly comfortable and they deflate into a small tube. I borrowed my daughter's sleeping bag, a mummy style rated at a temperature much lower than that in which I would consider riding a motorcycle.

I took the toolkit that came with the bike, augmented with a pocketknife, and a yellow flashlight that could be used as either a conventional flashlight or a lantern. Personal gear included a canvas shaving kit with the basics, and, of course, a towel. I took a college-ruled spiral-bound notebook and a ballpoint pen, as well as AAA maps and campground guides of the states I expected to pass through.

I started out with a heavy single-lens reflex camera and three lenses. I found I seldom used the camera and replaced it enroute with a lightweight autofocus camera with a zoom lens, which I still didn't use very much.

Since putting on my ratty old helmet was like going into the Buffalo Bills locker room after a Super Bowl game, I bought a brand new one, white because I thought it might be cooler in the desert.

The only other things I took were clothing. Including what I wore, I packed:

6	Polo-style shirts (all cotton mesh)
3	pairs of jeans
6	pairs of undershorts (boxers are more comfortable on a bike)
6	pairs of cotton socks
1	pair of thick-soled hunting boots (for riding)
1	pair of slip-on shoes (for camp)
1	pair of summer gloves (most of the time)
1	pair of lined midweight gloves (in the mountains and Alaska)
1	jean jacket (most of the time)
1	leather jacket (for cooler days)
1	rainsuit (absolutely essential)
1	lightweight sweater (later replaced with a couple of turtlenecks and a heavier sweater for Alaska)
1	set of longjohns (used only in Alaska)
1	pair of swim trunks (for lounging around the pool while I waited for my laundry to dry)

That was it. No radio, no tape player, no books. Everything fit comfortably into the saddlebags except the tent and Thermarest pad, which went on the luggage rack.

So, aside from equipment, how does one plan a trip like this? I had no idea, so I didn't. I would head east to the Atlantic, south to the Mississippi Delta, west to the Pacific, and north to Alaska, deciding in the morning where I would go that day. I would ride only two-lane or narrower country roads. And I would avoid all big cities and tourist attractions.

My wife Margaret would meet me in Houston for the Fourth of July, and again in Olympia, Washington. These week-long mini-vacations proved to be a great help in keeping me focused on the ride. And they gave Margaret a chance to share in the adventure. I never could have done the trip without her help and understanding. This sounds like the obligatory spousal statement but I mean it.

Once the motorcycle was purchased, preparing for the trip only took a few more days. I found myself alone at home most of the time, feeling vaguely guilty about not being at work. I had a long list of things I should have been doing around the house, but I could not get started.

We had done a lot of remodeling in our other houses, but when we moved here, we gave up. Of course, we dealt with the basics like painting, attic insulation and ventilation, new windows, and other repairs, but the kitchen and bathrooms stayed in their original form. The study never got built, and the screened porch was never enclosed to make a year-round room. I was too busy at work. We didn't have the money. Our needs were changing. So now that I had the time, I was going on a motorcycle trip. Forget the house.

I started reading literature again. Dusty books with stiff spines and yellowed pages unopened since my college days. Joseph Conrad. Mark Twain. Thoreau. And other authors I discovered in the bookstore. Barbara Kingsolver. Cormac McCarthy. Bruce Chatwin.

I began keeping a journal, experimenting with language. Asking impossible questions. Writing inadequate answers that I quickly discarded. At least I was experiencing things again, emerging from the long tunnel of my business career and stumbling about in the sun.

At first the stillness of suburban winter days was comforting, but soon it turned into a profound feeling of isolation. I needed to get back among people, so I volunteered as a docent at the George Eastman House International Museum of Photography. In the middle of winter there were few visitors, but those who came were knowledgeable. I spent hours in the galleries looking at images, excited by the wordless understanding that comes from viewing great photography.

Last fall, as I was winding down the business, Margaret and I attended a workshop at the Rochester Zen Center. From the street, the Zen Center looked like all the other well-preserved houses in the elegant, old Rochester neighborhood, but inside it was like Buddhist temples I had visited in Japan. It had the expectant stillness of sacred places and the resonance of hard spiritual practice. The simply crafted interior was highlighted by ornate altars with gilded statues of Buddhas and Bodhissavas glowing in the dim light. This was the traditional Buddhism I knew from my childhood in Hawaii, not some funky New Age stuff. Austere. Disciplined. Mysterious. Silent. I felt an immediate connection.

My parents, who grew up as Buddhists, became Christians in response to the strong missionary movement in Hawaii. I suspect that their wanting to succeed in Western society had as much to do with their conversion as religious conviction.

But my grandmother, who lived with us, was a Buddhist all her life, and she went to the temple every week. She knelt before an altar in her bedroom every morning and every night. The altar contained a lacquer shrine with doors to close off the Buddha figure inside. There was a photograph of my grandfather, who I had never known. An incense pot. Candles. And an offering, such as a flower or a perfect piece of fruit or a pile of rice cakes. The altars at the Zen Center were the same except for the photograph.

We were introduced to Zen meditation in the afternoon. We sat cross-legged and counted our breaths. Breathe in. Breathe out counting one. Breathe in. Breathe out counting two. When you get to ten, begin again. No thinking. Just breathe. If thoughts arise, just let them go. I never got beyond two or three without a thought intruding. I was amazed how busy my mind was. No wonder I always felt tired.

Part way into the round, my legs began to cramp. But we were not allowed to move for 25 minutes. It was starting to hurt. I tried to slide my right ankle very slowly off my left thigh to relieve the strain. "No moving," said the monitor.

I was stuck and in serious pain. It felt like trying to hold a heavy weight for much longer than the muscles could bear. But at least my thoughts were focused. When the bell rang signaling the end of the round, I almost collapsed. I could barely stand to begin the walking meditation.

Despite the pain, I could see the value of quieting the mind, experiencing the present, and seeking my true self. We went to the regular sitting the next morning and began practicing. After a short trial, we became regular members. I was accepted as a student by our Sensei. When I told him about this trip, he said, "It will change your life."

Because the bike was brand new, I wanted to put at least 600 miles on it before I left, to get it beyond the break-in period and the first major service. And I hoped I might feel more comfortable on the machine by then. Whenever I went to the garage during the long end of winter, I sensed the height of the shrouded motorcycle. As the days lengthened and the time to ride approached, my worries increased. Would I really be able to handle the thing? Fear of my unknown ability, of my untested endurance, invested itself in the tall, ungainly machine.

I started riding on those surprising warm days at the budding end of winter, when it was still brown and hard and cold in the shadows. It was like a shrug to loosen the shoulders after a long session at a desk. Swinging my right leg over the unaccustomed height of the motorcycle, I balanced on my toes, raised the bike upright, and heard the sidestand snap out of the way. I felt the oil-shrouded metallic friction as I pressed my left foot to select first gear. Then rolling, relaxing as the motorcycle leveled itself before leaning easily into the turn at the end of the driveway.

My early rides were mainly through the neighborhood, as I got the feel of the clutch and gearbox and brakes. Then, as spring hazed the trees in a green mist and the first chemists came to prevent crabgrass and dandelion infestation, I started using the bike as a daily driver for errands and trips to the Eastman House.

As the days warmed into May, I began to ride farther out, taking back roads into the small towns and villages around the Finger Lakes and Southern Tier. Winter drains slowly into the earth around here. Green comes late in the valleys, and as flowers bloomed on the hill, the watery bottoms were brown and silent.

The week before I left, workmen were putting a new roof on the house. They spent most of the time on the roof, snapping chalk lines, laying out shingles, and fastening them down with an air nailer. The compressor was in the garage and when it cycled it made more noise than the nailer.

I'd been setting up the tent in the backyard when I realized I didn't have anything with me to drive in the stakes. When I returned from the house with a hammer, two of the men were holding the tent.

"It almost blew away," one of them said.

"Thanks," I replied, moving it back and staking it down.

They stood watching for a while, then one of them asked, "Where you going with that?"

"On a motorcycle trip. Three months. Up to Alaska."

"You riding that motorcycle in the garage?"

"Yeah."

"Man, I wish I could do that." There was desire in their voices.

From then on, when they took their breaks, the men sat and watched me work on the bike and we talked about trips and dreams of trips.

There is something about a trip that takes over the mind. The crew foreman, dark and deeply wrinkled by 23 years on roofs, told us about an automobile trip he had taken across country when he graduated from high school. He could have been talking about last summer. To save money, he had slept in the car, washed up in gas station restrooms, and eaten bread and cheese he bought at grocery stores in the little towns. He worried about the car because it used a quart of oil between fill-ups but it made it fine and continued to run for two years after the trip. If he could get another one like it today, he'd buy it in a minute.

One of the younger men told us about his brother, who had gone with a friend on a cross-country motorcycle trip. They had run short of money several days from home and started sleeping in public parks. One night it had rained, but they found a picnic shelter and slept on the tables, wearing their rain gear. They arrived home with their gas tanks on reserve and less than a dollar between them.

The stories were always of hard times. Of going to places made more beautiful by the glad harshness of the road. Of meeting people and walking with them on the edge. Experiencing life.

2

Setting Out

The morning I left was warm and clear. Two men had come in a special truck to install new gutters on the house. The machine that made the gutters was inside the truck and they came oozing out the back like a ribbon of toothpaste. The truck was set up in front of the garage so I had to wrestle the bike around all the activity. It glittered in the sunlight, the purple several shades lighter than I had seen before, almost blue.

I checked the saddlebags on the bathroom scale to be sure they were balanced, then took them out to the bike. I bungeed the tent and Thermarest pad to the luggage rack and went in to say good-bye to Margaret. She got her camera and we went back outside. I started the bike, put on my helmet and gloves, pushed into first gear, and rode out the driveway under the glassy observation of the camera lens. As simple as that. Beginnings are often mundane.

I was more worried than exhilarated as I turned onto Route 31 headed east because the motorcycle seemed even more ungainly with loaded saddlebags and gear on the luggage rack. I rode past the supermarket and wobbled to a stop at the traffic light, shifting consciously and so deliberately that each shift was a bit late. The result was a jerky and uncertain forward progress.

Only a mile down the road, I pulled into a green and white Hess gas station to check the air in my tires. I had to unload the luggage rack to get at the air gauge in the toolkit under my seat. The tire leaked so much air when I checked it that the pressure dropped too low. It took a long time to get the tires right and I even considered using this as an excuse to go back home, but it was a pretty flimsy excuse, so I got back on the road.

It was a classic early summer day in upstate New York. One of those days for which we endure winter. The new green glowed through the yellow light as though it were submerged in a tropical pool. Sometimes the landscape shimmered as the pool of light was rippled by the warm breeze.

My spirits gradually improved as the little worries about the motorcycle and my riding skills receded. I rode through Macedon and Palmyra, familiar small towns I had ridden to while I had been breaking in the bike. The towns were strung along the road. First a sign saying ENTERING MACEDON, then miniature golf courses, little strip malls with beauty parlors, and auto parts stores. Used car lots. Gas stations with attached convenience stores. A little farther on sat the town center, identifiable by a few more homes, giving it a neighborhood feeling.

As the road dove deeper into the country, the villages became more traditional. Neat houses and lawns rested beside the road. White churches. Newark. Lyons. Clyde. Savannah. Some towns so small they were little more than a break in the fields.

I turned south at Savannah and crossed over the NY State Thruway just after it ran through the Montezuma Wildlife Refuge. On the map the Thruway is like a crease across the forehead of the state. After collecting a ticket gaining access to this road, it is possible to cruise the entire landscaped, inoffensive, unrelentingly green way above 65 mph, stopping only to refuel and eat at modern, convenient, clean rest stops that have recently been upgraded and standardized. Eliminating, finally, any possibility of adventure.

I watched trucks approach the overpass slowly, then faster, and with a wild roar, they would shoot from below along a black ribbon that ran straight down a green groove to the horizon. Time is money, got to get on down the road.

I rode slowly down to US 20 and headed east. US 20 used to be the principal route across the state but the Thruway had turned it into a museum, a memorial to those days when automobile travel was an adventure, when people went motoring to see the sights along the way.

I saw old motels where you could park your car right in front of your room. Restaurants in little buildings with big signs on the roof. The remains of curio shops and gas stations, their signs faded but recognizable. I slipped happily back into the human countryside.

By now I was feeling much more comfortable on the motorcycle and my anxiety began to give way to delight. I splashed in the warm green light and rode respectfully through the little towns that sat like dignified old men resting on benches along a path through a park.

I stopped for lunch in Skaneateles, at the northern tip of one of the narrow glacier-carved lakes that give this region of New York its name. The town seemed to be developing into a resort area. There was a crisp, modern cleanliness to the restored buildings facing the lake. I parked the bike in front of a busy building full of boutiques and walked up the street carrying my helmet.

I remembered a bakery from an old trip here. It was famous because it was included in one of the first offbeat guides to American roadfood. The bakery was still there, but the front window was dirty and the interior needed paint. The cardboard menus were stained with grease and their corners were broken. The food was unredeeming and there were only a few people in the place. On the way out I noticed a new restaurant across the street with dark green walls, varnished oak trim, polished brasswork, and potted plants. It was busy.

Beyond Skaneateles the towns receded and the countryside opened into farmland. Abandoned buildings occasionally stood next to the road, ghostly farmhouses with broken windows and grass growing in the gutters. A few buildings had collapsed, their black, broken spines monuments to better times. There were even barns with genuine Mail Pouch Tobacco ads painted on one side. "Chew Mail Pouch Tobacco. Treat yourself to the best." Persistent and permanent, they were all that was left of the colorful and entertaining billboards that once lined this road in those days before reliable car radios. The barns had survived the drive to clean up the countryside, to rid the highways of commercial clutter. If I chewed tobacco, I would surely try Mail Pouch.

It was still early when I arrived at Glimmer-glass State Park. For my first night, I wanted plenty of time to set up. My campsite was a basic one, with no hookups for electricity and water.

I was warned not to pitch my tent on the grass to avoid damaging it. I had to stay on the gravel and dirt parking and picnicking area. It was the only time I was told to stay off the grass the entire trip.

Setting up the tent took less time than I expected. The tent poles are made up of short lengths of aluminum tubing joined by an elastic shock cord. A quick shake is usually enough to restore them to their eight-foot length. The poles thread through color-coded pockets in the tent and are arched to form a dome. I opened the valve on my Thermarest pad and it self-inflated. The sleeping bag spilled out of its sack into a soft silky bed. I was set up in less time than it usually takes to check into a motel and carry in your luggage.

I asked the ranger at the gate where I could eat and he suggested a place on a back road going to Springfield Center. I found this to be the best strategy for finding places to eat. The other campers usually don't know the area and they often cook for themselves anyway.

The place was a clean, bright, family-style restaurant frequented by local people. I sat in a booth upholstered in red plastic. The table before me had a small gold design on a white plastic background. A glass sugar dispenser with a chrome lid and a spout with a little hinged cap was on the table, alongside glass salt and pepper shakers, and a full bottle of ketchup.

The food was basic roadfare. I ordered the baked chicken special and it arrived on an oval plate, a half chicken resting on a nest of stuffing, its head buried in a mound of mashed potatoes with a puddle of gravy in its center. The vegetable came in a separate dish. Soft broccoli in a cheddar sauce. Stark white rolls, thin crusted and soft, came on another plate with pads of yellow butter sandwiched in waxed paper. There was, as always in these places, homemade pie for dessert.

After eating, I sat at the table writing in my journal and looking at the map.

I rode back to my tent just as the sky began to shade into evening. Still excited by the day's ride, I walked down to the lake. Big motor homes and trailers had lumbered up to the pristine shoreline, their awnings draped over the picnic tables provided by the park. They seemed to transform the place into a lonely suburban neighborhood. A flickering blue glow from some of the windows indicated the owners were inside. Only one young family was gathered around a table in front of their tent trailer.

I sat for a long time at the edge of the water. The evening calm had polished the lake and it reflected the red edges of the clouds like fading coals in an old campfire.

3

The East Coast

I woke several times during the night to adjust my sleeping bag, but otherwise slept well and got up early. The tent, slightly damp with dew, was almost dried by the time I returned from the bathroom.

I broke camp quickly in the birdsong coolness of the morning. An animal, probably a raccoon, had climbed on the bike during the night and left muddy footprints all over the seat.

After checking my map, I decided to have breakfast at the same place I had dinner. I didn't see anyplace in East Springfield, where I turned off the highway to get to the park. The next town was twenty miles away.

This time I sat on a chrome pedestal stool at the counter and talked with the waitress and a farmer who had come in for breakfast. The farmer had started cultivating three acres but it had begun to rain so he decided to come in for breakfast.

"Funny, it didn't rain here," said the waitress. She had blond hair and was wearing a white shift with a pink apron.

"It only rained a few minutes," replied the farmer. "But I thought it was going to keep going." He was dressed in a flannel shirt, bib overalls, and rubber work boots.

"I don't do much farming myself anymore," he said. "Only a few acres. Most of my land I lease out. I've been thinking about selling out and retiring to Florida. Someday."

The look of the man and his exuberance for farming, and the weather, and the hope of each planting made me doubt it.

Once off Route 20, the road reverted to a country byway, through black, freshly-plowed fields, smelling wet and dark. It was entirely agricultural, mostly dairy, with cattle dotting the green hillsides. After a while, the road began to climb into the Catskills. The green enveloped me, coming right to the edge of the road and crowding overhead. I lost the sky for a while and when I emerged into a clear space I noticed it was grayer, the clouds converged into a dark uniform mass.

The motorcycle felt different with the loaded saddlebags and I leaned gingerly into the curves. I soon found I had to relax or I ran too wide coming out and had to correct awkwardly.

A motorcycle is not steered like a car. Instead, it is aimed at a point beyond the curve. Turning is a natural thing, simply leaning over and letting the gyroscopic forces of the spinning wheels bend the bike's path around the arc.

It begins with a push on the handlebars in the opposite direction, causing the motorcycle to lean into the turn. The spinning front wheel finds a new horizon, levels itself there, and the bike falls away. It is an unconscious act, executed with absolute faith in the outcome. Done right, a turn is joyful. Done uncertainly, it is uneasy and sometimes frightening, like falling backward off a diving platform.

The towns had become white clusters of homes. Between them, small businesses were scattered along the road. Gas stations. Grocery stores. Used car lots. Restaurants and bars. There were no malls or shopping centers.

I was delighted and intrigued to see shamrocks and Irish names on signs. At Durham, there was an Irish Festival proclaimed for summer, but not yet underway. These were the Irish Catskills, like the Jewish resorts just to the south, but more subdued.

I stopped for lunch at a deliberately Irish-looking place, a weathered brown one-story roadhouse with a pitched roof. The doors and windows had beveled glass panes. Inside there was a bar to the left and a large dining room to the right. The customers were mostly older, probably retired, and the waitresses treated them with familiar respect. The food was simple and good. Prices were reasonable.

As I ran down into the Hudson River valley, the landscape opened and the gray light seemed to warm. There were more cars. Strip malls began to appear along the road.

A strong wind pressed down the river as I crossed on a high, four-lane bridge. I rode in the open, above the guardrails of the bridge, surrounded by a blur of speeding cars. Water flashed far below between the bridgework. Pushed hard by the wind, I leaned forward and stared at the end of the bridge, my body tight and focused.

Damn.

A biker on a glittering new Sportster pulled up next to me at a stop light just beyond the bridge. "Just come over the bridge?" he asked.

"Yeah."

"Some wind, huh?"

"Yeah," I said as we rode off. "Yeah."

It had taken me a day and a half to get across New York, a trip that would have taken four hours on the Thruway. I picked up Route 7 in Massachusetts, just above the Connecticut border.

The countryside was picture-book New England. Little white towns surrounding well-tended greens. Church steeples rising above lush maple trees. Covered bridges and rock fences. No tangles of weeds between the fields and rusting machinery left at the end of the last row cultivated.

Further south, elegant strip malls appeared with signs made of engraved wood with gold-filled letters. The stores were mostly boutiques and antique shops. Many real estate and insurance dealers. Dog grooming salons and delis that looked like they sold tins of beluga caviar. The houses looked newly restored behind smooth green lawns impossible for the colonists.

I turned off Route 7 at Kent and found the gravel road leading to Bob's house. An older couple came up as I rode in. They had the look of a couple who had been together for a long time, their gestures and speech merging until I did not notice who had said what.

"Hi, we've been expecting you. We're Bob's parents."

"He's at work, but told us to give you a beer and let you get comfortable."

Bob's parents were from Oklahoma and were on their annual visit, staying in one of the two houses. They were dressed in the neatly pressed, light-colored, casual clothing that signaled a comfortable retirement.

We walked down to a large deck next to the lake where I was introduced to their neighbor. Mary wore vivid blue and red make-up and dressed in a splashy summer print in defiance of her age. Despite the differences in style, they were good friends, having gathered on that deck every summer for many years.

I passed on the beer since it was early, and sat with them by the lake, listening to their voices gracefully playing their courteous score.

The group broke up to prepare for dinner. Not wanting to sit inside, I walked out on the dock with Bob's fishing rod and cast a spoon toward some reeds on the opposite bank. I worked the lure along the reeds and the edge of some lily pads, experimenting with the speed and depth of the retrieve. Water bugs creased and dimpled the surface, almost like fish feeding, but it was too early.

Bob walked down the dock, smoking a cigarette, and holding out his hand in greeting. He is one of those perpetually youthful-looking people, sandy-haired, and ruddy. He had gained some weight, but his style was unchanged.

We walked back to the deck as I complimented him on the place. He was surprised I had never been to visit when we'd lived nearby. I remembered him talking about working on the house, but that was a time of small children, corporate careers, and barely enough time to watch some football on Sunday afternoons.

My corporate years were a blur of work. Over sixty hours a week, including most weekends. At least a week out of every month on the road. An endless cycle of preparing for meetings, making presentations, and following up.

I had no sense that I was doing anything meaningful, that all my effort was making any difference. Still, I worked harder and harder. The money was good and a lot of people worked under me, so I had power. But it was mostly an ego trip.

Although I try to control it, I have always been a highly competitive person. The corporation became my playground and I wanted to win. I wanted to be noticed. I wanted to be trusted with the tough assignments. I wanted the promotions.

It was a game I could play and win. And by winning, redeem all my other failures, proving that I was not a loser, after all.

So when I made a presentation, I anticipated every question that could be asked. And if I was in the audience, I prepared as carefully as the presenter, so that I could ask good questions and propose thoughtful solutions.

I don't remember much about those years. I have no details, as though I never lived through that time, only read about it in a book. I recall only the list of job titles and corporate moves that defined my life. Analyst. Manager. Vice-President. Rochester, NY. Stamford, CT. Rio de Janeiro. Tokyo. Boston.

I lost touch with most of the people I had worked with those fourteen years. We were competitors and when we left the game, we quickly forgot each other. We had no cause, no common interest, no intensely felt history to bind us. We shared only our individual ambitions, which were not enough on which to found a lasting friendship.

Beer in hand, Bob and I sat on the deck as the lake flashed its last white light before sunset. He had been through a lot in the years since we last met. Burned out by corporate life, unwilling to go on hating to go to work, he took a buyout package and bought a small printing company.

He talked as though I had experienced it with him, saying he had paid too much for the company but was blinded by the desire to get out of the corporation. He was deceived by the owner's offer to continue in the business. Once the company was sold, of course, the owner's interest disappeared. It was a scenario I had witnessed often among my small business friends, that of increasing preoccupation with the business, then desperation, family estrangement, and divorce.

Over dinner we talked about Oklahoma and driving and the grandchildren. Talk to fill the gaps in our experience, to find a common ground. Bob's parents were curious about me but didn't ask, preferring, I think, to speculate. Maybe they thought not knowing was better after they had experienced the maelstrom of Bob's divorce and the bankruptcy of his business.

Bob and I talked until late about our corporate experience. About old friends, some still hanging on, others involuntarily retired or working at some other company.

When I started working, corporations were fortresses of job security. But by the time Bob left, layoffs were just another profit-making strategy. Bob told stories of people coming back from the weekend to find pink slips on their desk instructing them to pack up their things and report the next morning to the outplacement center at a different location. Not even a handshake and "Good luck!" from their old bosses.

Bob's kids survived the divorce, living in the same house they had lived in when we were neighbors. The twin boys were seniors and Bob said they had to go to State College because of the money. He said they were good schools and the kids accepted it, but then he sat quietly for a while, sipping his beer and smoking.

Bob expected to survive the bankruptcy. He had made a deal that reduced his payments to the previous owner. Making the payments had severely crippled the company and now that they were reduced, Bob could see how he could make it. His energy seemed to be returning and with it, his plans and dreams.

I slept on a couch in the living room. Bob was gone by the time I woke in the gray light. His mother was in the kitchen and offered me breakfast.

"We already ate but I can make you some bacon and eggs. Bob's dad wants to come over but he didn't want to disturb you." I imagined them sitting in the other house, trying to decide what to do as I slept.

We ate and talked while I nervously looked at the weather. I was headed to the Jersey Shore to see Gunner and his wife Min, also old friends, this time from the Navy. By the time we finished eating, a misty drizzle had started. I put on my new rainsuit and asked for a plastic garbage bag to hold my Thermarest pad.

The ruts in the gravel road out to the highway had filled with water. I rode on the high center of the road and felt nervous about not being able to reach the ground if I'd had to stop.

Route 7 south of Kent is typically slow and congested. The road winds along the Housatonic River, a famous trout stream now so polluted with PCB that no fish from the stream can be eaten. But fishermen still line the banks on opening day, warily casting their lines to avoid their neighbors.

Route 7 becomes a six-lane expressway in Danbury, a situation I could not avoid because of the unrelieved urbanization of the area. I wanted to get around New York City as fast as I could, even if it meant using the superhighway. But once on it I felt vulnerable, thrown down a gray chute surrounded by spinning truck wheels and cars spraying dirty mist. The hammering and shrieking of the trucks and the sucking roar of the cars was like a mad rock concert played by demons.

I stopped for lunch at Marcus Dairy, a famous motorcycle gathering place. I had not been here since the Danbury Mall had been built and had trouble finding the restaurant, its sign now overshadowed by an elevated highway ramp.

As I was parking and fussing with the gear on the luggage rack, a group of Harley riders came in, followed by a chase truck with their luggage. They were headed to Laconia for the classic motorcycle races. Since they had ridden in from New Jersey, I asked about crossing the Hudson River. They said I should go to Tarrytown and pick up the Garden State Parkway. In return, they asked about I-84 going north, having heard it was blocked somewhere along the way due to construction. We looked at their map and I suggested going up Route 7, which was slower but more direct.

Inside, I took off my raingear and sat at the long, serpentine counter that jutted into the room like fingers. There was a thick newsprint magazine on the counter called *Connecticut Women* that had hundreds of ads placed by women seeking companionship.

There was an associated but smaller magazine called *Connecticut Men.*

Originally conceived as a nonprofit social service, the popularity of the magazine had overwhelmed its founders. It was still nonprofit, but now required the founders devote their full time to it. There were lots of rules of engagement and careful screening techniques to insure against unwanted funny business.

"SWF, professional, slender, N/S, loves country living, sports, hiking, movies, skiing. Looking for SWM, professional, 38–46, with similar interests."

"DWM, 30, 5'8", 175 lbs, good values. Interests: motor sports, outdoors, movies. Seeking D/SWF, 26–34, mature, honest and secure, slim a plus."

All this in Fairfield County, where BMWs, Mercedes, and Volvo station wagons outnumber Hondas, Fords, and Chevys, and where the only pickup trucks you see have landscape or home improvement business signs painted on the doors.

The rain settled into a steady downpour as I entered the Garden State Parkway. My rainsuit kept me dry but my leather gloves were soaked. The pocket where I kept my toll money leaked, sticking all the bills together.

The line of cars slowed, then stopped, as traffic from Manhattan joined the weekend trek to the Jersey Shore. After two hours of constant, heavy rain, only inching past two toll stations, I gave up and stopped at a gas station just off the exit. An off-duty motorcycle policeman stood next to the door, carrying his helmet and raingear, waiting for his wife to pick him up.

"Is it always like this?" I asked.

"Every weekend in the summer," he said. "You're crazy to be out there in the rain."

"I've got no choice. I need to get to the Jersey Shore. What should I do?"

"Try one-and-nine. It clears out earlier."

After getting directions, I dribbled out to the motorcycle and rode through a quiet residential area to Route 1. It was just as slow, but the blinking neon signs and traffic lights provided a diversion from the gray monotony of the rain. It was better than the blank vegetation along the Parkway.

The gray day merged seamlessly into early twilight and I realized I would not make it to Gunner's before dinner. I rode into and parked at one of the hundreds of fast food restaurants that lined the road, happy to be off the bike for a while. I went inside and stripped off my raingear, making a puddle of water on the floor. The people at the counter and sitting in the booths looked curiously at me but said nothing. I got a cup of coffee, hoping it would warm me up. My collar and cuffs were wet where rain had leaked in.

The telephone was outside. After a brief consultation with Min, we agreed I could probably arrive between eight and nine.

Back on the highway, I saw lightning striking downward like great ropes thrown down the black hull of a giant ship. I couldn't hear thunder inside my helmet but I knew by the cold electric feel of the air that the lightning was close. Somewhere I had read that motorcycles get hit a lot by lightning and, like trees, they should be avoided in electrical storms.

Enough.

I saw a Day's Inn sign high in the air several blocks ahead. $29 rooms.

Good enough.

The Day's Inn was in a long, low, two story blockhouse-style building set squarely in the middle of a glistening black parking lot. A flat roof jutting out from the middle of the building marked the entry. Not much money was wasted on architectural detail, but the place seemed to fit its rough commercial surroundings, now polished by the rain and sparkling with the multicolored reflections of neon signs.

I parked at the entryway, relieved to be out of the rain. Inside, there was a slight scent of the Orient through the dampness. Sweet, not the usual plastic smell of budget motel lobbies. At the counter it came to me. *Mississippi Masala,* a film I had seen not long before, had been about an Indian family that ran a motel in the Deep South. It was the persistent, exotic perfume of curry.

I recognized everybody there, as though I had stepped into a scene in the movie. There were several young men. Serious, striving, making it in America. And in another room, behind the front desk, a matriarch sat in a purple sari with a red dot between her eyebrows, her gray hair pulled back into a bun. A darkly beautiful, intensely feminine young woman sat with her, dressed in western clothes.

"Do you want the telephone?" asked one of the young men who was checking me in.

"What?" I asked, understanding neither the question nor the accent.

"The phone. You need to pay a deposit if you want the phone."

"Oh, well, no phone, then."

After I filled out the form and presented my credit card, he took everything to the back room where a slim, intellectual-looking man studied them at a desk. New Jersey Masala.

The desk clerk came out the side door, surprising me. He beckoned down the hall and handed me the key. Perhaps he felt that trying to explain how to find the room was too much of an effort for my limited ear and his accent.

The room had a door opening into the parking lot behind. I parked the motorcycle where I could see it through the window, unloaded everything, shut off the fuel supply, and locked the seat, but I was nervous about leaving the bike unattended.

The room was clean and dry, if dated, as though it might once have been a Holiday Inn. I soon had my wet gear festooned over every piece of furniture.

There was a Chinese restaurant next to the motel and I ran across the parking lot in the drizzle, deflecting through a small used car lot whose wares were parked like obstacles in a pinball machine. It was a dimly-lit place, decorated in the classic red brocade, black lacquer, high-class American Chinese restaurant style. A waiter, dressed in a white shirt that seemed to glow almost blue in the dark room, came quickly to the table.

I had a vegetarian noodle dish that was more than I could finish. My fortune cookie advised me to keep my plans secret for now. I sat, sipping tea and writing in my journal, before going back to my room.

4

The Atlantic

I woke before my 7:00 a.m. call and was relieved to find the motorcycle had not been stolen overnight. I packed quickly in the monotonous gray light and rode out. There was little traffic on the road. It seemed as though all the cars in New York passed through last night, leaving the area empty. Although it was not raining, I wore my rainsuit against the spray from the still-puddled road.

The highway branched a short way down the road and I followed Route 9 south, onto the shoulder of New Jersey. The oily urban landscape quickly transformed itself into broad, open marshlands. The road was raised above fields that were still wet and white beneath the gray sky. Although I was no nearer the ocean than before, I could sense a saltiness in the air, a briny, seaweed smell.

To the east there were more scenic roads along the beaches. I imagined them curving along the rocky coastline with glimpses of nice houses situated to maximize the ocean view, and passing through little towns with boutiques and restaurants decorated with lobster traps and bits of rope. The road I had chosen was a working highway for the farms and cranberry bogs of the area, straight and purposeful and plain. It worked for me.

Gunner was in the front yard waving as I rode up. I had not seen him for many years and he was heavier. He wore a gray jump suit and a red ball cap with "USMC Retired" on the front. Gunner insisted I put the motorcycle in the pole barn where he had cleared out some space between some farm machinery.

We went in the back door of the house, through a mudroom with a washer and dryer, and into the kitchen where Min stood quietly. Min is taller than Gunner and has soft gray hair compared to his bristling military haircut. Her quiet, melancholy style exaggerates, and is emphasized in return, by Gunner's precise, energetic manner. They were so different, these two, that at first glance they seemed not to go together. She had lived all her life on the flat Jersey Coast, working at the telephone company while Gunner did his duty in the Marine Corps. The nomadic military life was not for her so she pondered the level coastal marshes while Gunner marched and polished and qualified on the Marine marksmanship course.

Gunner is a nickname given to Marine Warrant Officers, men whose technical skills earned them expert status. "Gunner" is sometimes confused with "Gunny," the nickname for Marine Gunnery Sergeants, the highest enlisted rank. It's like "Beemer" and "Bimmer," the first referring to BMW motorcycles and the second to BMW automobiles.

Long military service, constantly among young men testing their limits, bestows a grace and dignity upon a man that makes him instantly recognizable. It may be the posture, still alert and straight despite the beginnings of a paunch. Or the deferential manner that demands as much respect as it offers. Or the attitude that has succumbed to discipline and emerged the better for it. But you can always tell a career military man.

We were old friends, going back more than twenty-five years to when we rode cargo lighters up the coast of Vietnam and stood watches in the White Elephant Operations Control Center in Danang. That was a year that changed my life, and Gunner is one of the icons of that time.

As we ate lunch, we enjoyed our ritual litany of the people we had served with and exchanged what we knew of their present lives. Commander Reiber made Captain and retired to the Washington, D.C. area. Gunner kept up with him and occasionally visits. Commander Collins, whom I followed, made Rear Admiral before retiring and was now consulting in Japan. We spoke of these men with pride in their accomplishments, happy to have known and served with them. It was a feeling I had become unfamiliar with during my years of corporate rivalry.

I wanted to see the Atlantic before I turned west. It was where I wanted to begin my trip, a symbolic starting point. The beginning, midpoint, and end of journeys are not geographical locations but states of mind, and although I had not overcome all my uncertainty, I was ready to begin the ride. I felt now that I would not turn back until I got to the end of the road in Alaska.

Riding in the familiar confinement of Gunner's car, we occupied ourselves with conversation until we drove out on a narrow spit of land. We parked, and as I got out, I felt the open possibility of the ocean. We walked out onto the broad beach, grayer than the sky and littered with scraps of seaweed and worn plastic. Houses, some of them on stilts, lined the flat shore. They had a temporary feel, well back from the water but still vulnerable, their builders unwilling to invest in more permanent structures.

The water was gray and white where it reflected the sky. There was only a dim horizon, a darker gray line that could have been either ocean or sky, softly lying on the rounded edge of the earth. I walked along the beach, picking up shells then returning them. I wanted no physical remembrance of my having been here.

Headed west, at last, I felt no anticipation or worry. No need to plan or prepare. No uncertainty. Only the unheard roar of the ocean behind and the unseen horizon ahead.

5

Southwesterly

The morning was Atlantic gray. Listless light drifted into the room, promising an overcast day along the coast. I was anxious to leave so I resisted relaxing into the kind of conversation that could have kept us sipping coffee all morning. The excitement of beginning was muted by the dull day, but I was happy to be setting out.

The roads in this part of New Jersey are a gigantic grid. Divisions of land are precise rectangles bounded by straight roads. All the turns are ninety degrees left or right, sharp-cornered and flat. There are no hills or mountains to bend the roads, just the coastal flatness of new land made by the waves and rivers, of sand and silt. Unimpeded by nature, man was able to civilize the land, imposing order, regularity, and the efficiency of straight lines and right angles.

I found my way through the grid onto a four-lane highway leading to the Delaware River Bridge south of Wilmington and settled easily into the rhythm of the traffic, feeling confident and secure after having survived the water torture two days ago.

Suddenly, the engine stumbled and restarted itself. "Shit," I thought, "What now?"

The engine stumbled again and died. I coasted onto the paved shoulder of the road, my mood quickly dimming to match the sky. I cranked the engine a few times with no luck. Gray worry faded into black despair. With the bike on the sidestand, I sat on the Armco barrier gazing at the purple pile of junk. I sat for several minutes, with cars and trucks thumping by every few seconds, thinking my ride was over before I had even begun. So much for legendary BMW reliability.

It was an effort to rouse myself and begin the time-honored ritual that everyone who has ever ridden British bikes has learned to perform automatically:

1. The thing cranked, so the battery was okay.

2. Ignition. Check the spark. I pulled a plug wire and cranked the engine. A long thread of lightning ran to the cylinder head. Okay.

3. Fuel next. I looked at the petcock. It was in its usual position.

Ah.

Idiot.

Dumb, Dumb, Dumb.

I had run out of gas.

I had forgotten to fill-up in all the rain-sodden misery two days ago. I sat back down on the Armco barrier humiliated, embarrassed, and relieved. Adventures are such fragile things it is a wonder any of them get beyond the dreaming stage.

Most motorcycles do not have fuel gauges. The rider approximates the gas supply by setting the odometer to zero after filling the tank. For example, I know my bike gets 45 miles per gallon and has a 5.7-gallon tank, meaning I have a range of about 250 miles. When I get to 200 miles, I need to start looking for a gas station. My odometer showed only 180 miles.

But long periods of idling (0 mpg) and stop-and-go riding like I had done the day before will lower your gas mileage and decrease your range. Motorcycle manufacturers have taken this into account by installing a petcock that leaves some gas in the tank when it is in the normal ON position. When the tank runs down to the reserve level, the bike seems to run out of gas and quits. Switching the petcock to RES releases the remaining gas in the tank, usually providing enough fuel to find a gas station, about a gallon, or 45 miles of normal riding. It is a simple and elegant alternative to complex and unreliable gas gauges.

I turned both petcocks to RES and started the motorcycle.

I skirted south of the humming Wilmington metropolitan area and was quickly into the rolling Maryland countryside.

The air was cold and I stopped to put my sweater on under my leather jacket. Wind-chill is a real threat to motorcyclists when the temperature drops into the '50s. Every inch of skin must be protected from the rough-edged wind.

The chill was sharp and deep, finding chinks in my protective clothing. It was a gray, miserable cold, like a pinch just before you need to scream, sore, but not unbearable. The mind, too, must be set against the cold wind, lest it drift into some warm and dangerous reverie. I tried to focus on the cold, to discover its misery, to surround and extinguish it. It was hard and fatiguing, like performing manual labor all day. And despite all my effort, it was still damn cold.

I chose to follow the thinnest gray lines on the map except for a short, unexceptional section of US 1 from Rising Sun to Hickory. There are two US 1s in the country, one on each coast. The highway numbering authorities, in their political wisdom, chose to give both coasts the first highway. Could you imagine California accepting number two? Have you ever seen a Second Baptist Church? Anyway, there is not much chance of confusing drivers although it's possible somebody has set out on US 1 in San Francisco thinking they were headed to Boston.

The countryside was familiar, and riding through it was like hearing a favorite tune on the radio. I knew the music well but it still engaged me.

I stopped for the night at Codorus State Park in southern Pennsylvania. The campground was empty and I got a grassy campsite on the edge of a large field that could well have been a Civil War battlefield. A fire would have been nice, but I had no equipment, not even matches. I settled for a warm dinner at Clair's, a country restaurant alone on a rise overlooking open hayfields.

It was cold the next morning as I set out across the rest of Pennsylvania. Shortly after leaving the campground, I passed through Gettysburg. It was a small village, very neatly reconstructed. Modern, despite the deliberately colonial buildings. I sensed clean, white-tiled bathrooms lurking in all the buildings, all conveniently placed and clearly marked.

There was an agricultural haze in the air, and the morning light was lemonade-shaded. Low hills lay ahead, green up close, then black, then fading into the gray horizon in precise steps like a photographer's gray scale.

It was dairy country, exceptionally neat and planted alternately in stripes of hay and corn, some of the hayfields white and others brown or green. Giant toilet paper rolls of hay were scattered about the fields.

I got to Ohiopyle State Park late in the afternoon and was directed to a campground on the other side of the park. The road began a steep drop into a narrow valley and I could see the road coming out above me as I descended. At the bottom was an abrupt, off-camber, first-gear switchback advertised by skid marks all over the road. I went in nose-down, braking hard, and leaning on the handlebars to keep from sliding forward. A second later, I came out head-up, sliding back on the seat. The bike had run through the turn easily.

The campsite was not as good as the last night, just a large, grassy field with picnic tables scattered about. But I was relieved to be finally out of the cold wind.

On the way into the restaurant that night I stopped to admire a '50s vintage Norton Combat Commando parked next to the door. Norton, like all the other British motorcycle manufacturers, had gone out of business, unable to compete with the Japanese, who built reliable, inexpensive, and efficient machines. Still, the British had made motorcycles that glittered with chrome and polished aluminum excitement. Machines that defined the audacious simplicity of motorcycling. No windscreens or plastic bodywork, just two wheels and an engine, each part polished and unambiguously purposeful. Like an athlete's body, no excess and shaped by its use.

The Norton rider came to my table after I sat down. He had come to the restaurant for a cup of coffee, but it had been just an excuse to ride the Norton.

"The bike's in restoration," he said, "but it's rideable." It was an unnecessary apology, made to establish his standards.

"Looks perfect to me," I replied.

"Nah, the handlebars and controls are screwed up. The guy that owned the bike before changed them. He thought he was upgrading the machine. Damn parts are hard to get now-a-days, so I left the old bars on so I can ride."

I thought of the stark honesty of the Norton. Real motorcycling. Noisy, unreliable, uncomfortable, dangerous enjoyment. I was momentarily ashamed of the BMW I was riding. It had an electric starter and a small fairing that kept the wind off my chest.

Then I recalled the British bikes I rode in the '50s and the vibration that numbed every part the body that touched the bike. It was so bad it even numbed my adolescent sex drive. The BMW is smooth and quiet, and I get off at the end of the day feeling fine. Besides, these days I need all the sex drive I can get.

The next morning was still cold coming out of Ohiopyle, but it warmed as I rode south into West Virginia. Prosperous farms in Pennsylvania, white clusters of buildings set in green fields, gave way to neat roadside homes with big lawns, some fenced. Then clapboard bungalows with gravel drives. More pickup trucks than cars, and those were mostly big, old American models. Then mobile homes with white aluminum skirts, decorated with lawns and flower gardens. And, suddenly, steep hollows and worn houses built right on the edge of the road.

It was like standing before a gathering wave, drawn into the increasingly rural countryside, then struck by a green wall, twisted and pumped by the road. Forget north, south, east, and west. Appalachia has only two directions: up and down. The roads were fabulous. Great curves and switchbacks hanging off the edges of the mountains. My only concern was approaching cars. There were not many, but when they came, they were usually a surprise.

Steep valleys crowded the houses to the roadside and there seemed to be no level land to cultivate. Small, tough, rural towns began to pop up. Not neat villages, but worn places, some nearly abandoned. The churches were well tended, however, and looked prosperous.

I rounded a curve and came on a roadside rest area with a shelter, picnic tables, and clean restrooms. Just below was a small stream that I could hear singing in the country quiet. No cars came by the entire time I was there.

The green of West Virginia was close, almost in your face. Rough, weathered green like old Army fatigues. I had gone only a short distance south and the pastoral green of the Northeast had been replaced by foot-stomping, mountain green.

I had planned to take a break once a week and had already been on the road for seven days. Glenville State Park was un-crowded and I found a good spot off to myself where I set up for a two-night stay.

The motorcycle, however, always attracted attention. Two students from a local college were drinking beer and cruising the park in a big, old, beat-up Chevy coupe. They drove over to my campsite and one of them called out, "Hey, where you from, buddy?"

"New York."

"Wow, where you going?"

"Out West."

"Wow, I sure wish I could go with you."

"Tough luck."

"Hey, you just missed the Fiddler's Convention. Last week-end this place was jammed full of people. Everybody just hootin' and hollerin'. We came every day. Ain't much else to do around here."

"Too bad for me."

"Hey, you want a beer?"

"No thanks, I got to ride back into town for dinner pretty soon."

"Okay. Hey, see you later." They drove off to cruise the rest of the park.

For a college town, there weren't many places to eat. I had dinner at an Italian restaurant stuck between a supermarket and an auto parts store in a little shopping mall just outside of town.

It rained hard that night, the rain drumming hollowly on the fly. I woke and thought about getting up to check but went back to sleep. The alarm woke me at 6:00 but I didn't get out of the bag until 7:00. It was my first good night of sleep on the ground. The air was rich and moist and cool.

I had breakfast at a black and white diner on Main Street. A glossy checkerboard linoleum floor. Black stools and chairs. White countertops and tables. White walls with black trim. A color TV, tuned to the weather channel, was predicting more rain. I had the special, biscuits and gravy with home fries, $1.15. Coffee was 35 cents.

Afterward, I walked down the street looking for a Laundromat and found half the storefronts empty. A dim antique store occupied a vast space that must have once been a department store. It smelled damp and musty as I walked by, the ancient scent crowding the sidewalk in front of the door. Further down there was a thrift store with racks of clothes, tables piled with dishes and some old appliances. Next to it a liquor store, "Moonshine. Not over 30 days old. Shine on Kentucky Moon."

I found a laundry on a side road leading to the college that washed clothes by the pound. I left my things with them after making sure it wouldn't cost more than $5. It cost less than $2 and they folded everything neatly and wrapped it up in clean paper.

The other end of Main Street, where I had parked, had a Pizza Hut and two gas stations with convenience stores. Old men dressed in worn flannel shirts, overalls, and ball caps, sat on benches along the street. They stared silently as I walked by.

At the corner, an old man sat on a cardboard box, his back resting against the wall of the gas station. He had a can of beer in his hand. The rest of the six-pack was on the ground in front of him, still fastened together by the plastic holder. We nodded to each other as I passed.

I rode to the college, which seemed to be glued to a green wall, the brick buildings stacked behind each other up the steep mountainside. Looking for the library, I went in the ground floor of one building and walked out the back on the third floor.

There were no students around so the library was quiet and empty. Only an occasional shadow, perhaps a faculty member doing some research, suggested the normal activity of the place. The sleepy green drizzle outside seemed to warm the building.

I wrote in my journal and sat quietly most of the day. I had no desire to read newspapers or magazines. I looked at the books in the open stacks surrounding me but did not take any of them down.

A lot of trivial worries had fallen off somewhere back down the road and my greatest concern had become taking the next curve smoothly, experiencing where I was and what I was doing. Stay in the present, I thought. Just ride the motorcycle. If there was any value in what I was doing, it was in discovering just how full the present could be.

It was still raining the next morning, so I got my rainsuit on, packed everything wet and rode out.

Ohio happens suddenly at the border, where patches of level fields appear. The dense, vertical wilderness of the mountains civilizes quickly into neat farms and grass-enclosed homes along the road. It was like a calming sea after a storm, the steep waves smoothing into gentle swells, their tops rounded, then eventually flat, and I felt I was riding the slanted edge of the wave down into the center of the continent.

The shit-kicking country music playing at the West Virginia Dairy Queen where I had eaten lunch had given way to Muzak at McDonald's.

Late in the afternoon, I found myself along the Ohio River and far from any listed campgrounds. I passed a trailer park that advertised camping so I turned back and went in. It didn't look promising, with mostly big house trailers permanently parked on a grassy field next to the river. There was nobody at the manager's house next to the road. Only a small dog barking wildly when I knocked.

On my way back to the bike, a pickup truck pulled up. "Looking for a place to camp?" asked the driver.

"Yeah."

"I think the manager is setting up a trailer. He should be back soon. Hop in, you can wait down at my place."

We drove down a gravel road beside some scraggly looking corn. "Pretty sorry looking corn," I said. "Must have been lousy weather this spring."

"That's not corn," he laughed. "It's tobacco. They pinch it back all season to force the leaves to grow. Those plants will be five feet tall by the end of summer. Then they cut it and hang it up to dry in those barns."

He stopped and pointed at a curious looking hut with what seemed to be enclosed porches on both sides. The vertical siding was so loosely nailed that I could see through the building. "What they do is bundle the tobacco stalks, tie them to frames, and hoist them up in the rafters. Come on, I'll show you."

We got out and walked into the field. "Everybody used to have a small tobacco field around here. They're not too big because the plants need tending all summer and you have to chop and dry them by hand. Of course, now people think it's too much work. The money is still pretty good, though, $2,000 an acre."

Over the years, the bare wood of the barn had achieved the rich color of tobacco and I smelled the sharp scent of old memories. Of Zippo lighters. Ashtrays with restaurant logos. Smoke rings that grew a yard wide before fading into the blue-layered barroom haze. Cigarettes with coffee or scotch whiskey. Smoking used to seem more romantic than disabling and deadly.

On the way back, we saw some children near a pen by the roadside looking at a fawn that the manager had been given. The children's mother sat in a big Chevy with the finger-streaked windows rolled up tight. She waved four plump fingers at us as we passed.

The manager, who had a speech defect as a result of a mild stroke, said, "Set up anywhere. Pay later." He had difficulty getting the sentence to start, then the words came out too rapidly, like a breached dam. People talked to him in a loud voice, as

though he were deaf, and often answered their questions themselves while he struggled to respond. But he was well-liked, probably because his speech defect forced him to listen more than talk.

Later that evening I found myself in the middle of Manches-
ter at what appeared to be the only restaurant in this one-street
town. I parked the bike next to the restaurant and took off my helmet. A group of kids were waving at me from across the street and
I waved back. But they continued to wave their arms and shake
their heads back and forth. They were warning me of something.
I looked around and there was nothing. Then I pointed at the restaurant. They nodded and pointed up the street I had just come
down. The restaurant I was about to enter was no good and I was
being sent to one I had passed before entering town.

I got back on the bike and the kids cheered as I rode off. I
must have escaped something truly awful, because the other restaurant was a Dairy Freeze with a limited full-meal menu. Unfortunately, I was unable to experience Tom's Genuine Stairway to
Heaven Spaghetti because I'd had a gout attack the night before.

After dinner, I sat with Kelly and his wife, mother, and father
around a driftwood campfire close to the river. People passed on
the way to the dock and everyone stopped to talk. The evening
was clear and cool and I felt almost alone despite the people and
house trailers around. The stars shone blue behind the yellow
sparks rising from the fire. Green and blue lights from the occasional pusher boat glowed on the river and faded.

As usual, we traded stories about motorcycle trips, the rides
becoming more and more difficult in the telling.

Suddenly, Kelly's wife asked, "Why are you taking this ride, if
they are all so tough?" It was the only time I was asked "why?" the
entire trip.

"I don't know," I said. "I thought I knew when I started but I
really didn't. Anyway, I haven't been gone that long." I didn't
know and didn't care to know.

The conversation quickly swerved around this philosophical
landmine and we were soon back to flat tires and running out of
gas and the virtues of Honda Gold Wings.

The Ohio was strong. Big, slow, full of mist and glittering waves, the water green and gray and brown. The pusher boats drummed by all night, their sound rising and falling like tides. I lay in my tent and listened to them come up the river. First a melodic hum like a cat's purr growing to a pulsing Latin beat more like a rumba than a samba. Not loud. Steady. Then accompanied by a splashing fountain, the song sometimes echoing as it passed by my tent.

Northern Kentucky was all about grass and money. Dark horses grazed on green meadows enclosed in white fences, enveloped in an opulent haze of wealth and leisure. These playgrounds were like golf courses, but more subdued, and in that way more exclusive and lonely. I saw no actual people there, only the rich evidence of their occupation of the land. The wealthy do not play along the road. I guess they need to hide from the resentment of the rest of us.

Southwest of Lexington, horses and money give way to cattle and dairy, with big rolls of hay in the fields. It was still grassy, but rough-edged and working.

After a week on the road, my mind began to lose its focus and I caught myself following random thoughts drifting through my head. I struggled back, over and over again, back to The Ride until it became a mantra, my reminder to pay attention, to stay connected. The Ride was everything, the road, the experience, now.

I rode on US 62, an old two-lane road that paralleled the four-lane divided Bluegrass Parkway, but far enough away to put me into the countryside and relieve me of its manicured monotony.

Hungry and seeking to avoid the fast food chains infesting the section of the highway close to Lexington, I stopped at a tiny diner on the top of a low hill. Except to use the bathroom, I refuse to stop at the McDonalds, Burger Kings, Kentucky Fried Chickens and other plastic and neon national chains. Since they are everywhere, however, they have helped relieve many an otherwise pressure-filled ride.

This was a real diner, a railroad car with a long counter down one side and narrow booths on the other. Nostalgic yuppies had not yet discovered it and the place exuded a greasy aura, its chrome and glass dully reflecting years of honest use. The menu consisted entirely of burgers, hot dogs, and a lone tuna sandwich, which I ordered with a Pepsi.

The man running the griddle was sitting at the end of the counter. He had sun-bleached hair and his skin was burnt and darkened from hard outdoor use. He looked awkward and almost embarrassed wearing a stained white apron.

The only other person in the place, a woman with simple, quiet features, made the sandwich from soft, white bread and pulled the Pepsi from an old-fashioned dispenser. She put the sandwich and drink on the counter.

"Where you'all going?" she asked.

"Out West."

"I used to ride with my husband. We had a Kawasaki 650." I wondered if the man at the counter was the husband.

"We quit riding because of the traffic. It got so bad around here, you know. We almost got killed a few times so we just gave up the motorcycle."

"It's not so bad."

"No, it's really dangerous nowadays. You better be careful."

When I paid up, the woman said, "Now you take care. Ride safe."

I passed through Bardstown, where an old friend had grown up. We had been roommates in Vietnam and later attended the same graduate school.

Bardstown happens suddenly. I rode into a suburban area, with homes spaced closer and closer together as I approached the town. Then I seemed to pass through a gate into an open square, the center occupied by an imposing building with a distinctive civic authority. I knew instinctively it was a courthouse. Surrounding the courthouse, on the other side of the street that ringed it, were low office buildings. The square had a sense of self-containment, a place with limits.

I rode around the courthouse looking for a place to buy a Coke and found only law offices, stationery stores, and a couple of restaurants. It seemed the only thing the center of town offered anymore was justice.

On the street leading out the west side of the square I saw a grocery store. As I walked in, I noticed the windows were gray with dirt and obscured behind heavy, rusting, metal screens. Inside there was a small group of people lined up at the counter. A lean black man in worn overalls bought some cigarettes. Behind him a woman with a child on her hip and two more attached to her faded print skirt, all of them about the same size, bought a small bag of groceries and paid with food stamps. She had a tough, defiant air.

As I paid for my Coke, a couple of white men wearing jeans and worn pocket T-shirts stepped behind me. Other than necessary exchanges at the cash register, nobody said a word. I was relieved to get outside with my Coke. I sat in the sun next to my bike and drank as I watched a few more poor-looking people go in and out of the store, few leaving with any bags.

I camped that night at Wax, about twenty miles off the highway on a man-made lake. It was clean and far enough away from Mammoth Cave National Park to be relatively uncrowded.

The restaurant across from the park entrance advertised all-you-can-eat catfish dinners, so I decided to try it. The restaurant looked out over a small marina with houseboats and pontoon boats docked in precise ranks along long finger piers.

A young boy, no more than 12 or 13, showed me to a table, gave me a menu, and brought a glass of water. Since I was having the catfish dinner, I put the menu aside and began to write in my journal.

A pleasant woman came to the table and said she would be right back to get my order. I had written several pages before I realized I had not ordered. I tried to get the woman's attention but she was rushing around the other tables in the now-filled restaurant.

I managed to get the attention of the boy and asked him if I could order. He said, "Just a minute," and left. He returned after several minutes with a pad of paper and a pencil.

"Just give me the catfish and iced tea," I said.

"Okay," he said. He brought back a glass of iced tea.

A half hour later, after several refills of iced tea, I was still waiting and my mood was worsening. I trapped the woman who was serving and asked if I could get my meal.

"Oh," she said, "What are you having?"

"Catfish."

"Be right back with it," she said.

Another half hour later, the boy brought a plate containing two small catfish fillets surrounded by greasy-looking hush puppies. I was almost finished eating the catfish when the boy returned with a dish of cole slaw and a basket of rolls. This was turning into the meal from hell.

The woman returned and asked, "Do you want more catfish? You can have all you want."

"No, just bring me the bill, please." I waited another half hour.

It was an intensely leisurely meal, challenging all the equanimity I had accumulated so far on the trip. I guessed that there were only three people working in the place that night. A husband who cooked, a wife waiting tables, and the boy who greeted me, who must have been their son. I think they were new at it and were clearly over their heads.

As I was leaving, the woman asked, "I hope everything was alright."

It wasn't, but I couldn't tell her that.

Breakfast cost 62 cents at a boater's gas stop near Wax. I sat on a bench outside and drank coffee from a Styrofoam cup and ate a round, glazed pastry in a cellophane wrapper.

A little boy came up. "Is that your bike?"

"Yeah."

"Wow, it's great."

A business suit came up. "Are you 'touring'?"

"Guess so."

"I used to ride a Harley to college in New Mexico. Every year."

"From here?"

"Yeah. Never went 'touring' though. Hey, ride safe."

"Thanks."

Riding through southwestern Kentucky, the sky got bigger. High, thin clouds made patterns of folded lace on the western horizon. The land receded from the sky and fewer hills interrupted the fields. Golden brown wheat fields appeared on one side of the road, and expanses of green corn on the other side. It was the first break in the relentless green of the East.

6

The Mississippi Valley

The road flattened in Tennessee. Almost no throttle adjust-
ment was necessary to take the rises. The roads are drawn
with laser-like precision between the towns, straight and true. The
countryside became Southern, with red dirt and dark green pine
trees. Black people driving dusty, clapped-out old Chevy and
Ford sedans. Hot.

At the end of the day, I came to Interstate 40, to one of those
exit villages made up of gas stations, fast food restaurants, and
motels. Since I was nowhere near a campground, I decided to
spend a night off the ground at the Comfort Inn.

I ate dinner at the Western Sizzler across from the motel. It
was my first meal in days that was not breaded and deep-fried.
But I was uncomfortable in the powerful air conditioning and left
right after eating.

In the motel room, I shut off the air conditioning and opened
the windows. The room looked away from the highway so the
noise wasn't too bad.

Was there a time zone change someplace around here? I had
had an extra hour's sleep by my reckoning, but didn't feel any
more rested. I felt polluted. Too much to eat last night, plastic
fumes in the room, the bed too soft, and the noise from the highway.

I rode away feeling that the Southern accents around the
highway stop had seemed contrived, almost theatrical. I heard it
from women wearing dresses just a bit tight, showing a little roll of
fat at the waist. I heard it from men considering automobile maga-

zines at the convenience store rack. This was a shopping channel, polyester jump-suited, microwaving, Cadillac-yearning, string-tie accent, spoken at Interstate exits by people on the move. It seemed a bit incongruous under the familiar logos and in the universal architectural design of the big chains. There was nothing else at that exit village that was Southern except the map coordinates and the voices. Funny, once back in the country, I no longer heard such aggressive accents.

The gas stop this morning was hard South. Pay before you pump.

Inside the convenience store, a thin white woman balancing a child on her hip bought pancake syrup with food stamps. The cashier sat in a wire cage surrounded by cigarettes.

Out to pump. Hot. Back in to get change. A large black woman traded food stamps for gas money. A man paid more than $2 for a quart of oil. High prices and suspicious service. Barely making it.

I got screwed up outside of Memphis and found myself riding into an upscale suburban area with landscaped development entrances displaying tasteful names ending in "Pines" or "Woods" or "Estates" or "Manor." Neat shopping malls clustered at intersections. Coming out of hard country, it felt artificial.

Clean, shiny, Mercedes, Saabs, and Ford Explorers were on the road, accelerating quicker and braking later, only to wait longer in the clogged Sunday morning church traffic. I kept the bike rolling slowly to avoid putting my feet down.

Looking for a way out, I rode into a strip mall and stopped next to a black and white police cruiser. The power window glided smoothly down as I rode up and a large pot-bellied trooper gazed out at me through dark aviator glasses. A shotgun stood on the rack next to him.

"I'm looking for a way to get to the river without going through Memphis," I said.

"Were y'all from?" he asked.

"New York."

"Okay. You best take 302 over to 61. I live down that way, right on the Mississippi line. But you be careful once you get on 61, it's a dangerous highway. Lots of accidents there."

He pointed down the road and said, "302 goes off to the right after you cross the state line. It's marked."

I was quickly over the border and into Mississippi. The transition was abrupt, the road suddenly hardening into the country road I had been on earlier in the day, with red arcs on the pavement where dirt side roads intersected.

Next to the river the land was flat and fertile and hazed out to the horizon, the gray rising to a small pale blue dome exactly overhead. Heat shimmered off a road that went straight to the fuzzy horizon. It was humid. Moist. So agricultural you could feel the fertilizer-crazed plants panting like athletes on steroids, their steaming breath forming a green veil over the fields.

It smelled fertile, like that first shovelful of soil when a hole is dug. Sometimes it was the eye-watering, sweet aroma of manure, sometimes it was bitterly hog-scented. Distinctive, strong smells. A green smell in the glowing light seemed to come from nowhere in particular.

The road ran on and on, straight, flat, and otherwise featureless. But, to me, it was full and entertaining.

The parking lot in front of Campbell's Famous Bar-B-Q in Tunica, Mississippi, was filled with big American cars, a good omen for hungry travelers. Inside there were mostly large, laughing, black families, the men dressed in neat denim overalls and the women in colorful cotton dresses. A few small, somber white families looked like they had just come from church, the men wearing suits and ties and the women in pastel dresses.

I walked to the counter in back and ordered a barbecue sandwich for $2.99, a mound of pulled pork in tomato sauce, topped with finely-chopped cole slaw, encased in a soft hamburger bun. There was Louisiana Hot Sauce on the table and paper napkins in a battered black holder. The air was smoky.

I crossed the river south of Greenville and continued falling south through Arkansas and Louisiana. Approaching Lake Bruin, sudden curves appeared in the road. Gray wisps of Spanish moss hung in the dark green trees. And the levee to the left, a low, mislocated hill, held back the river.

I set up camp at Lake Bruin State Park. Coming out of the tent, I found five kids lined up looking at the motorcycle. They were ranked by height, the oldest a girl about fourteen on the left, down to a boy about six or seven on the right.

"I like your bike," said the oldest.

"I like your bike," echoed the youngest.

"What kind is it?" asked one in the middle.

"A BMW."

"Where did you come from?" asked another middle.

"New York."

"I went there once," said the oldest. "To a modeling competition. I really want to go back." I looked closer and saw potential, still fuzzy with baby fat, but with the kind of bones that could support a genuine beauty or at worst a pretty face.

"I like that color," she said. "Purple is my favorite color. Look, my T-shirt is purple. Everything I have is purple." The other kids started squirming and glancing knowingly at one another at the egotistical turn in the conversation.

"Where are you going?" asked a middle, trying to save things.

"First to Texas, then across to California, and then up to Alaska."

"Wow!" I could feel their longing for travel to new places, for great adventures. Their imaginations roamed fearlessly across the country, seeing things that only the free minds of children can see. I wished they could simply go, like I did. I knew that by the time they were old enough, they were likely to be overwhelmed by caution and trapped by commitments.

We gathered around the picnic table and looked at the maps and talked until they had to go back to their family picnic. They all lived nearby and said repeatedly that there was little to do except watch TV.

Laura, the oldest, gave me her address and asked me to send her a card from Alaska. This set off another attack of squirming and glancing and they all left, running and waving goodbye.

The park ranger I asked about a restaurant said there was nothing nearby but I could go over to the Lake Bruin Grocery and get a mighty fine po' boy sandwich. I was met in the dirt parking lot in front of the wood-framed store by Tim, who was sitting on the porch as I rode in. He came over as I parked and took off my helmet and jacket. He was a genuine good old boy, red-faced, paunchy, and boisterously friendly. Curious, full of talk and love for the area, he quickly learned where I was from and where I was going.

"Come on in and I'll get Tom to fix you right up," said Tim.

Tom, the gray-haired, tanned, and deeply wrinkled owner, took me back to his barbecue. Every weekend he smoked pork loin, beef brisket, and homemade sausage (all homemade, including the hog) in a gigantic black iron smoker. There was a rich, almost sweet smell that Tom said was pecan wood.

Probing with a long fork among the bones and sausages, Tom said there was not much left by Sunday night, but enough to make me a po' boy. I decided on the brisket and he mounded a paper plate several inches high with chunks of meat and placed a fat sausage on the rim. Tom made some space on the plate by mounding the meat even higher and added a large spoonful of potato salad from a tub in the refrigerator. Two token slices of white bread on top completed the sandwich. Tom wrapped the whole thing in foil and we went out front.

Tim was talking with a frail lady at the cash register. "You got quite a trip going," she said. "I can't get around much on account of my game leg, but I've been a few places. I went to see my daughter in LA a couple years back. Hoo, you should see the traffic they have out there!"

"While you're here you ought to go to Nachez to see the old homes," said Tim. "And to Jackson on the New Roads Ferry. It's one of the last ferries across the Mississippi and it's still free. You know, Jackson was the original capital of Louisiana. It's real interesting and real old."

I got out my map and Tom showed me how to ride on top of the levee, down to New Roads. "I chopped cotton all down through there," he said.

The sunset colors over the lake matched the intense heat of the day. Night was only marginally cooler. Fireflies moved against the black shrubs, mimicking the immobile stars above. One firefly on the ground blinked furiously. Two armadillo clanked through the brush at the edge of the campsite. Rain later cleared the air.

The next morning I rode beside the levee to St. Joseph, looking for a place to eat. The town was huddled at the base of the levee, the grass-covered hillside forming an improbable backdrop for the low buildings.

The St. Joseph Café was a worn old place with a wood-framed screen door that banged shut as I entered. My nose and eyes puckered at the smell of vinegar and raw onions. A white-haired woman sat at a table chopping onions and adding them to a white enamel tub full of cucumbers. There were no other customers in the place.

"Bread and butter pickles," she said as I passed.

A large black woman brought a cup of coffee. She wore a colorful green, white, and red dress, and a red apron. There were rings on all her fingers, some with two on the same finger. Silver bracelets piled halfway up her left arm jingled softly as she moved. Cajun?

Another black woman wearing a blouse of the same colors brought my eggs. Both women had soft, melodious voices that seemed to rise at the end of sentences to just short of a question, before rounding back down to a period. I found it difficult to understand but pleasant to listen to.

In the deserted morning heat, Nachez had the feel of a town that was trying hard to get into tourism but had not quite made it. Everything focused around a roughly-restored marketplace with restaurants, souvenir shops, and a horse-drawn carriage terminal for rides through the historic neighborhood. With so few people around, there was a feeling of anxious expectation, like a shopkeeper waiting for his first sale of the day.

I rode through the well preserved, but not quite restored, historic district. Some of the houses looked honestly old and worn.

Either that or I had gotten off the carriage tour into the "real" Nachez.

On my way out, I stopped at a roadside park along the Mississippi. Although I had been riding next to the river since Memphis, this was my first good look at it. Yesterday, I had paid $2 to go into a county park to see the river and had even climbed the observation tower, but it had been too far away. This view was free, which was good, because it was not as impressive as I expected, just a large brown body of water more like a lake than a river. I missed feeling the power and movement I knew was there. But these things take time and I needed to keep moving. So, disappointed and a little frustrated, I pushed south.

Back on the west bank of the river, I rode on top of the levee. The floodplain reached to the river on the left and little towns passed below on the right.

The rain began so suddenly that I was drenched by the time I got my rainsuit on. There was no cover on the top of the levee. I rode for a short distance but couldn't see more than a few feet ahead and got onto the shoulder mostly by feel where I sat on the bike to wait it out. I worried about passing cars not being able to see me, but only one pickup truck went by, and it was just creeping along.

The downpour quickly abated, but a steady drizzle persisted as I rode on. I spotted a roadside gas station/grocery/bait shop, and rode in under the gas pump shelter. An older man with a white crew cut sat on a bench in front of a tan Cadillac Eldorado drinking a beer hidden in a paper bag.

"Looks like you got pretty wet there, buddy."

"Yeah, it rained so hard I couldn't see."

"Why don't you leave the bike there to dry off. They won't mind."

"Okay." I went inside for a cup of coffee and asked the woman at the cash register if she had any sandwiches.

"No," she said. "But I can sure make you one." I went back outside to wait for the sandwich and sat down on the bench next to the old guy.

"I'm retired from the Navy," he said. "That's why I'm drinking beer in the middle of the day. It's my hobby."

The Chief described his retirement life as driving either his Cadillac or his motor home to the grocery most days to drink beer and shoot the shit with people that dropped in. He often brought the motor home because he thought the cops wouldn't suspect a motor home driver as much. Plus, if he got stopped, the cab was high enough that the cops couldn't smell his beer breath. Sometimes, he said, he took his girlfriend fishing on his boat but he didn't like to fish himself.

"I was in the Navy, too," I replied. "Seventh Fleet aboard the USS Chipola and on the beach in Vietnam."

"I was in Saipan and Okinawa in WWII, did minesweepers during the Korean War and Subic Bay during Vietnam. I made Chief Yeoman and got out after 30 years."

"Guess you did liberty in Olongapo, too," I said, closing in on the common ground.

"Yeah, a cold San Miguel was the best damn thing in the world when it was hot like it got back there."

He hailed a young man with a short military haircut that made him look like he should still be in high school. "Hey," he said. "This is Bobby. Bobby, meet Lt. Notch. Bobby is in the Navy, too."

We listened as Bobby proudly told us the classic young seaman's tale of drinking San Miguel beer in Spain, "Man, was I fucking drunk. I was so shit-faced I couldn't stand up to go take a leak."

Ah, I remembered those days, going on liberty in the Philippines. Spending the afternoon at the officer's club, getting up a head of steam. Heading out to our favorite bar in Olongapo. Laughing and talking. Becoming the heroes we wanted to be. Then suffering through the next few days at sea, recovering from the poison of cheap beer.

Drinking was part of one's attitude in the Navy. We were young men trying everything. Testing our limits. Wanting to be part of the group. But my civilian drinking had been different. I drank to relieve the relentless tension of corporate life and to mute the feelings of envy, distrust, and anger that grew out of the intense rivalry.

It was easy to develop a drinking habit. I relished the smoky bite of single-malt scotch. The ceremonial opening of vintage burgundies. The musty scent of ancient port. A pint of bitter in comfortable wood-paneled pubs in London. Giggling hostesses pouring sake in tiny clubs in Tokyo. Happy hour. The relaxation following the first sip. The camaraderie. The escape.

For a while, I commuted to Los Angeles almost every week. I always stayed at the Marina del Rey Hotel and drank at the hotel bar almost every night. After I arrived one Sunday night, I went to the bar. The bartender put my usual bourbon in front of me. I looked at the glistening amber liquid, smelled the inviting sweetness, and asked, "Can I have a beer instead?"

I have not had a drink of hard liquor since then, but at the time all I did was substitute beer and wine for martinis and highballs. I bought cases of beer and jugs of cheap California wine instead of bottles of scotch and bourbon. I still drank too much, but it was cheaper.

I began to worry when episodes of not remembering what happened the night before became more frequent. I had known people who had drinking problems and had seen how it had corroded their lives. Did I have a problem? Maybe. I knew that once I started drinking, usually at parties where the liquor was abundant, I often overdid it. So after an especially bad night, I quit altogether.

It was easier than giving up smoking. Social gatherings were the toughest. I wanted to drink to be part of the group. But I hung on, watching everyone else get loose, remembering what it was like after a bad night. The urge slowly faded. I held out for almost ten years, until I was well out of the corporation.

I started drinking again a year ago on a personal trip to Japan. I could not resist an Asahi Super Dry beer with the barbecued beef dinner we were cooking at our table. And I had a ceremonial drink of sake to celebrate the New Year, served in an overflowing wooden box with a pinch of salt on one corner.

Since I started drinking again I have managed to stay under control. But I have gotten close to losing it at parties. Not like my vintage years, but close enough to make me worry. Now that I am completely out of the game, am I safe? I don't know.

The rain eventually quit and I headed out with directions from the Chief to a store on the way to New Roads. He wouldn't tell me why I should stop there, only that it would be worth it.

I found the store on a side road, a small, low building like most of the little grocery stores in the area. There was a covered porch along the front, with worn benches along the wall.

Inside, the light was bright enough to see, but seemed dim because of the dark walls and ceiling. Low shelves lined with colorful grocery labels filled the room. The ceiling was supported by exposed beams on which hung deer trophies, hundreds of them, antler to antler, covering the entire room with a blanket of death. There were deer heads on the walls above the grocery shelves, creating a bizarre and eerie ambiance.

Everywhere dead eyes glittered and sharp antlers protruded. Soft brown fur, some with white stripes along the neck, blended with the dark beams, as naturally camouflaged as the living animal. As my eyes slowly adjusted, revealing more and more detail, my mind recoiled in shock.

A picture window on the back wall looked out to a pasture in which a herd of deer grazed. The living animals so intensified the feeling of death and despair in the place that I quickly turned and fled.

7

The Delta

I stayed in St. Francisville at a small commercial campground that surrounded a muddy pond. There was a swampy, dark green, slightly sulphurous smell emanating from the black shadows, spicing the dim afternoon light.

The rain began again that evening and in the morning I had to pack the tent in a soft, steady downpour. But being wet or dry no longer seemed to matter. I was getting deeper into The Ride. Not taking pictures. Not visiting historical sights. Not gaping at natural wonders. Not logging another attraction on the tour. Just riding.

On the way to Jackson the sky cleared briefly to the east and there was sunrise at 10:30, a gold sky and yellow-tinted clouds, the lightness rising above a black mountain of clouds. By the time I reached Jackson, the sky had closed to a uniform gray and the warm rain had resumed. I spotted a '50s-style drive-in and decided to stop for lunch.

As I struggled out of my helmet and rainsuit, making a puddle on the floor, a large man, weighing more than 300 pounds, watched me intently from the next table. He wore a red bandanna around his thick neck and a large white T-shirt that stretched tightly across his belly. He had a short, stringy beard that circled his chin, accentuating the size and roundness of his large head. He slowly poured Coke out of a liter bottle into a paper cup. In his hands, the bottle looked normal-sized and the cup looked like one of those little ones out of a water-cooler dispenser. The overall effect was ominous, and I thought about getting back on the bike and finding another place to eat.

"What are you riding?" he asked.

"A BMW," I said, warily.

"What kind?"

I wasn't sure how to answer since he didn't look like a motorcycle enthusiast, but I said, "an R100GS."

"I've got to go out and look at it," he said. He rose, revealing his impressive height and girth, and maneuvered out the door.

I ordered the catfish po' boy and coffee breakfast special, even though it was closer to what I thought of as lunchtime. Daily events seemed to slip later the further south I went, perhaps to avoid the steamy intensity of the day's heat.

Bill came back in and invited me to join him at his table. "I really want one of those new GSs," he said, turning over a pile of motorcycle magazines. "Look, it was reviewed in *Cycle World* this month."

I leafed through the magazine but it really didn't interest me.

"I went on a diet once and got to be just as slim as you," he said. I was dubious, but said nothing.

"I knew it wouldn't last so I got a small bike, a Honda 350, while I could enjoy it. I really had a good time with it. Now, of course, I'd need a big machine."

His knowledge of motorcycles was broad and accurate, so I had to take him seriously. We talked about motorcycles long enough to establish our mutual respect, then turned to other subjects.

"You know," he said, "People are afraid when they first look at me. But when I tell them I am a nurse, it's okay." Bill was a nurse at a mental hospital. His size was an asset with some of the more unruly patients.

It turns out that Jackson is really best known for its mental hospital and maximum-security prison. So much for its history as the original capital of Mississippi.

Bill rolled his own cigarettes using French paper. He thought Italian was better but was impossible to get locally. He put five kinds of tobacco in his pouch, but didn't mix them, so each cigarette tasted different. "You do whatever you can for excitement in Jackson, Mississippi," he said. "The only other exciting thing that I can remember was, once, John Wayne ate in this very restaurant. They were shooting a movie around here and came in for lunch."

"If it was John Wayne making a movie, it had to be a long time ago," I said.

"1964."

I wanted to go further into the Delta before heading to Houston, so Bill pointed out a route that would take me through what he described as the "epicenter" of Cajun culture. He also suggested I stop at the biggest Honda dealership in the world in Baton Rouge. Since I was avoiding cities and didn't ride Hondas, I figured I would pass.

Bill came out to hear me start the motorcycle. I knew he was listening to his longing to ride in the syncopated beat of the boxer's engine.

Jackson had a shabby elegance that could be glimpsed down curving driveways and between overgrown plantings in neglected front yards. Old, columned houses stood erectly among ancient trees like still-proud Confederate soldiers. The vegetation was dense, dark green, and tropical, filtering the rain in drips to the black forest floor.

On the way out of Jackson, the rain forest abruptly opened into cleared fields, some partially flooded. Cattle grazed on the high spots and there were no trees to break the view. A steel mesh fence topped by coils of razor wire ran next to the road. Another similar fence stood behind it, and finally a long wall. The prison. The open areas between the fences were live fire zones for shooting escapees.

I stopped along the road. The plain walls, fences, and open fields seemed to darken the already gray day. It was a malevolently desolate place. A community of outcasts, raging together. A van full of prisoners passed. All of them turned to look at me, freedom on every mind. They had the same look that ended almost every encounter I have had on the trip. If I could have heard them, they would have said, like almost everyone else, "I wish I could do that."

Here, criminals were imprisoned by walls and the force of arms. Nearby, there were people imprisoned by their minds. And everywhere, there were people imprisoned by their lives.

The ride south turned very wet after I left Jackson. As I approached Baton Rouge, I noticed my faceshield flapping and water leaking into my helmet. The screw holding the left faceshield mount had vibrated loose.

I stopped at a store and bought some duct tape, the modern replacement for baling wire and universal motorcycle emergency repair part. As I was checking out, the kid at the register told me about a motorcycle dealer a few miles away that might have helmet parts. He came to the door with me and asked, looking at the bike, "How fast will that thing do the quarter mile?"

Outside, another kid running through the rainy parking lot shouted, "I like your bike!"

The dealer turned out to be the place that Bill had told me about. It was in a gigantic warehouse-style steel building. There were hundreds of motorcycles arrayed across the showroom floor. The place felt empty on this rainy afternoon and all the salespeople had retreated to cozier nooks and corners. I found the parts counter and although they didn't have the right part, we were able to jury-rig a repair. It was not great cosmetically, but it worked.

Pushing deeper into the Delta, the rain intensified and I hit flooded roads. In White Castle, I stopped when I saw the road disappear under a muddy puddle of water. Some kids in soaking T-shirts were happily splashing in it. A few adults trudged through on the sidewalk, holding green and yellow rain slickers above their heads, the water just above the ankles of their rubber boots. I could see the road come out the other side, about 50 feet away.

What the hell, go for it. I put the bike in gear and rolled into the water. Within a few feet, my footpegs went under, then my boots. Oily steam rose as the hot exhaust pipes hit the water. The GS has a high mounted muffler and exhaust outlet to allow for fording streams and the motor ran fine even as the lower half of the cylinders went under.

The kids cheered as I rode steadily through the puddle, the bike making a steaming wake like a powerboat. This sucker was a lot deeper than I thought. I had forgotten to allow for the curb height. Then I was through, the bike rising from the puddle like a scuba diver walking out of the water.

And I found myself laughing inside my patched-up helmet, loving the rain and wet roads.

I saw sugar cane and flooded fields that could be rice. Then the bayou appeared, small houses perched over the water and houseboats moored along the shore. People living as close to the water as they could get. Seafood, shrimp, and crawfish for sale in roadside stands.

The rain created an early darkness. Lightning began to paint the sky and I followed directions to a nearby motel advertised on a billboard. Rooms were $33. I dined on crawfish estoufee at a nearby Cajun restaurant recommended by the desk clerk, so I didn't even have to get back on the motorcycle to eat.

I rode toward Texas in the morning. It was clear, but the damp air still carried the memory of last night's heavy rain. Then an onshore breeze began. The sweet sea air, washed by miles of Gulf water, pressed hard against the bike. The agriculture shifted from sugar cane, to rice, to pasture. Closer and closer to Texas, the land dried out and its palette changed to red and brown. Once over the border, it was all parched brush and weeds.

I was headed to Houston, and as I approached, the traffic intensified until it reached full urban stress levels. At various times, the highway exploded into soaring interchanges with frighteningly high and windy overpasses. There was also a long unexpected tunnel that I rode through half-blind at 65 mph, because I could not remove my sunglasses or slow down for fear of being hit from behind. Cities are not friendly places for motorcycles.

Part 2
The West

8

Houston

Relentlessly suburban, Houston spreads like an oil slick over the level landscape. Neat, ranch-style houses on lots a bit small, but providing adequate privacy, rest in green subdivisions with gently curving streets to disguise their repetitive monotony.

The subdivisions are bounded by wide, straight boulevards with strip malls and gas stations at every intersection. The boulevards lead to freeways that connect to other subdivisions, office campuses, and major shopping malls.

Houston is a city based on the automobile. There is plenty of parking. It's efficient. It's clean. It works. If we are not careful, it could be our future.

Yee-Min was standing in the driveway when I rode up, waving both arms and jumping up and down excitedly. Margaret came running out of the house carrying her camera. She had flown into Houston the day before.

"Welcome, welcome!" cried Yee-Min. "I thought you were lost. Were my directions okay?"

I put the kickstand down and raised my helmet visor. "Hello, Yee-Min."

"I told Yee-Min you wouldn't get lost," said Margaret. "You rode 3,000 miles and didn't get lost."

"It's hard to get lost if you aren't going anyplace special," I said. "But I didn't have any trouble finding your house."

We first met Yee-Min and his wife Gin-Chi in Boston. Yee-Min was a graduate student at the Massachusetts Institute of Technology. We were part of an organization that befriended foreign students, partly because we remembered being newcomers in a foreign place, but mostly because we enjoyed being around younger people with different perspectives.

They had a daughter, Alice, and a son, Roger, who was born at MIT while they lived in student housing, a gray concrete apartment building where the halls smelled of cooking grease and exotic spices. Their apartment had had a tiny kitchen built into an alcove next to the front door. It was always cluttered with pots, pans, and food containers. In that kitchen, Gin-Chi had produced some of the best Chinese meals I have ever eaten.

Gin-Chi's face was marked with a childhood complexion problem and she dressed like a college student, but there were wedding pictures in their apartment that showed her as glamorous as a movie star. Done by a skilled fantasy-maker, the pictures still seemed appropriate. They celebrated a future as clear and radiant as their parents' hope and their own promises to each other.

Things worked out just as they hoped. Yee-Min got his PhD and green card and was now a research chemist at Phillips Petroleum. Gin-Chi was a real estate agent selling homes to up-and-coming Chinese families. They lived in a nice Houston house, bigger than most, in an upscale neighborhood. Yee-Min drove a mini-van because the kids needed the space and Gin-Chi had a white Lincoln Town Car she used to drive her customers around. They were well into the American Dream.

We spent a week in Houston and, by the end of the time, I could feel the comfortable inertia of the place weighing on me.

We went to a Fourth of July rock concert in a local park and found the grounds carpeted with beer drinkers. The blue Port-a-Potties that dotted the lawn like icebergs in a rocking sea of colorful T-shirts were doing a brisk business. Near the bandstand there was the scent of burning hemp. We settled for a place out of the action and far enough away from the loudspeakers to minimize the pain.

We made the obligatory visits to NASA and the San Jacinto Battlefield. Mission Control was closed to the public due to an active space mission, but the rockets on the lawn were impressively phallic. San Jacinto, where Sam Houston defeated Santa Anna and broke the grip of Mexico on Texas, had been turned into a historic park complete with an admission fee, a multi-media slide presentation, interactive museum exhibits, and clean restrooms all located in a new, air-conditioned building that seemed too cold. Outside, informative signs pointed out key features of the site, like the neatly mowed lawn where the battle took place.

Yee-Min made Chinese dumplings for us one afternoon, rolling rice dough into discs like small tortillas, folding them over to enclose a tablespoon of stuffing, then cooking them in a frying pan.

He had not changed much over the years. He was heavier, not fat, but prosperous-looking, like a lean version of the good luck figures on the checkout counters of Chinese restaurants. He continued to exude a happy, self-contented energy, leaning forward as he spoke and laughing often. His voice was always high and excited, as though he were playing a game, which of course he was.

9

Texas

It was difficult getting started again after Margaret left. I took an extra day to change the oil and wash the bike. I wanted to get back on the road, but I had gotten used to the secure comfort of Houston. Leaving was like that hesitant moment at the beach just before diving into the ocean. I know it will be refreshing, but I always cringe just a little beforehand.

Early the next morning, I rode southwest, following the wide boulevards out of the city to avoid the jammed freeways. I was quickly out of the sprinklered suburbs and on State Route 36 headed northwest through the dusty industrial edge of Houston. Pastel steel buildings surrounded by baked asphalt parking lots. Chain-link fences with bits of paper and plastic debris caught in the wires. Occasional incomprehensible piles of junk and parking lots full of strange machinery. The structures standing alone. An empty, level place.

A marquee sign on the side of the road advertised The Best Inn Restaurant, which specialized in Seafood, Chinese Food, Steaks, Bar-B-Que, Chicken Fried Steak, and the Best Egg Roll. Clearly a multi-cultural establishment. The parking lot was full of pickup trucks, a good sign.

Even though it was early for lunch, I decided to stop. Inside, the rich smell of barbecue was stirred by ceiling fans. No air conditioning. The tables mostly filled by working men wearing jeans and cowboy boots.

There was a counter in back where the food was served cafeteria-style. Mounds of meat and fried chicken in steel trays. I saw no Chinese food, although the owner and cook were Chinese men who obviously understood that success was based on giving people what they want.

I ordered a sliced beef sandwich, a mound of beef on a bun, painted with a deep red sauce, delivered on a Styrofoam tray. I walked to the front and sat at a Formica topped table with a chrome napkin holder, a greasy saltshaker, and a half-filled bottle of faded orange Texas Hot Sauce with a dark crust around the red plastic top. Good.

After lunch, Houston disappeared quickly and I was into vaguely familiar countryside. It resembled the cowboy serials I used to watch on Saturday afternoons at the Golden Wall Theater, only greener than I had expected. The movie serials were a child-hood ritual when I was growing up in Hawaii's pre-TV era. It was important to get there early to get a seat in the balcony because popcorn often rained down on the kids in the pit during the gushy scenes. Like when Roy Rogers kissed Dale Evans.

We watched Hopalong Cassidy or the Lone Ranger riding through the dusty countryside chasing desperadoes. Our imaginations soared in the big sky of the prairies and sat by the lonely campfires after a hard day in the saddle. When the movie was over, we went outside to the shocking green hills and valleys, the towering banyan trees, and the fragrant scent of plumeria and hibiscus.

By the time I reached the campground at Lake Somerville, I had regained the familiar aches and pains of the ride. I had a friendly, comfortable ache in my right wrist from holding the throttle open and a burn in my buns that I relieved by standing on the footpegs.

The park ranger at the gate explained why things seemed so green. "We had so much rain this year the lake flooded and the park was damn near all under water. It peaked this spring at 16 feet above normal. It's still 11 feet above normal and lots of camp-sites are under water. But you can probably find something. There're not many people here."

The view from my campsite included the tops of several submerged picnic tables and the upper half of a restroom facility. Except for these signs, the place looked normal.

I had dinner at "The Country Inn—We Specialize in Beef." It was crowded. Most of the men were dressed in crisp blue jeans, Western-style shirts, and cowboy boots and hats. The women wore neat print dresses. If they were not so unselfconscious, I would have thought they were a bunch of yuppies on their way home from line-dancing class.

The reason for the popularity of the place was its steaks. The small sirloin weighed in between two and two-and-a-quarter pounds. I had the smallest steak they offered, a big, juicy one-pound rib eye that reminded me of the beef we used to eat in Brazil, almost as tasty, but not as tough. The beef at The Country Inn came from a local ranch and was probably grass-fed. Almost all U.S. beef comes out of feedlots where it is fattened on grain and confined to a pen to keep it tender. The result is virtually tasteless. A ripe tomato is a more rewarding culinary experience.

Back at the campground, I sat at the picnic table with my journal as the sun reddened the sky over the black lake. It was a comfortable and familiar feeling. But, as I began to write, I found myself struggling to describe the day's ride.

My language was leafy, green, surrounded by trees and mountains. In my language, it was necessary to climb to high places to see very far. But here it was open and windy. All I needed to do was to raise my eyes to see vast distances. I liked the endless reach of the low horizon, measuring myself against the infinite dome of sky, feeling the hopeful emptiness of the grassy prairie. But I needed a new vocabulary to describe it. A level, almost spiritual vocabulary. A dusty, sand-textured vocabulary. An earth-toned tan and red and yellow vocabulary. Because the West is brown.

The next morning I had a Dolly Parton sighting at breakfast. There were three women sitting at a round corner table. One of them, Dolly, got up as I walked in. She wore a floral print dress and makeup that was a clearly a statement, not a cover-up.

She showed me to a table where I had a good view of the group and gave me a menu. "The girl will be with you in a minute, honey."

The girl, dressed in a blue waitress uniform, came over tentatively with a glass of water. She was nice, but plain in comparison to her boss.

The other two women at the table with Dolly were also in full battle dress. One wore a light blue denim jumpsuit with rivets around the collar. The other was wearing tight designer jeans (not bad for her age) and white old-style tennis shoes. It must have been their regular morning coffee session. I imagined them going home later and sitting in fringe-curtained living rooms watching their favorite soap operas.

For a while I was the only customer. Then two men came in wearing cowboy boots, long-sleeve Western shirts, and Wrangler jeans. One had a ball cap and the other, a cowboy hat that they both kept on the entire time. They nodded hello to me and teased the women gently before settling down to their coffee.

Riding northwest into the heart of Texas, the landscape flattened out and dried to a yellow-brown blur at the bottom edge of a gigantic blue sky. It was hard to imagine the sky getting bigger, but every day it did.

The comforting green embrace of the hills and valleys and trees of the East had disappeared completely and now there was only sky in all directions, clear overhead, then filled with ghostly wisps, then an afternoon forest of clouds on the western horizon. An endlessly moving, changing, restless sky. This was a place for nomads.

The wind was a physical presence, an invisible force constantly pushing, bumping, rubbing, wearing. Sometimes I seemed leaned over for hours, relieved only by the wind shadows of trees or a low hill. Tractor-trailer rigs stirred the air for a mile behind them, making a bumpy mess to ride through.

Mid-afternoon I stopped at a roadside picnic spot to rest and drink some water. I lay down on the smooth concrete table with my jacket for a pillow and was asleep within seconds. I woke an hour later, stiff but refreshed.

I camped in a state park again, but this time the park was full. The motorcycle drew a lot of small kids with questions but only one adult came over to talk.

The ranger at the park recommended I try the Country Oaks for dinner, but on the way into town, I saw a lot of pickup trucks parked in front of the Kountry Kitchen. It was all-you-can-eat catfish night. They start you off with three big catfish fillets, hush puppies, and fries. It made a mound six inches high. Cole slaw, lemon wedges, tartar sauce, and pinto beans came in small bowls. Few people requested seconds.

The sunset on the prairie was brilliant, big, and red. It was also abrupt, extinguishing quickly into night.

The next morning I stopped for gas in a small prairie town that first appeared as a bump on the horizon. I parked the motorcycle at the pump and was taking off my helmet when the owner walked out of the service bay wiping his hands on a rag. "What kind of bike is that?" he asked.

"BMW," I responded, expecting to answer the usual questions about the motorcycle, like how fast it would go and if it was comfortable to ride all day.

"It looks like an enduro," he said. Hmm, this guy knows what he is talking about. "I have a Gold Wing. My son and I are going off for a week on it, leaving next week."

"Great."

"But I'd rather be doing what I think you are. Just riding around. On the loose. That's my dream. Someday."

"I'm headed to the coast and maybe up to Alaska."

I pumped the gas and walked to the office for the cold Coke the owner offered. We stood in the shade of the building and talked about what I might run into on the Alaska Highway. He thought my machine was well-suited to the task, but worried that his Gold Wing might have a rough time.

A dusty pickup truck stopped in front of us and the driver asked, "Is this guy doing what we have been talking about for years?"

He was an artist and had driven all over the southwest looking for scenes to paint. Several years ago the simple pleasures of motorcycling caught him and now he wanted to ride. The two of them talked endlessly about breaking out, but I didn't think anything would happen until one of them just took off on his own.

I am trying to keep this journey unstructured. Although I know generally where I am headed each day, I try not to worry about the particulars. I just follow the road, stopping wherever it interests me, minimizing my planning and all associated decisions. I could not have done this during my goal-oriented, decision-obsessed business life. But out here on the prairie, it seemed like the only way to travel.

I used to plan our family vacations in great detail, accounting for every day. But nothing ever went as planned. So we suffered through the poor directions and the wrong turns. The attractions that seldom turned out to be what the guidebooks described. The full parking lots. The long waiting lines. The impatient kids. The unexpected price increases. The lost reservations. Always rushing to the next stop. Always late.

We returned home with lots of pictures but no memories other than the time we got lost and spent a whole afternoon driving around aimlessly, causing us to miss the performing seals described in the guidebook. Or the incredible traffic jams at the national parks whenever the goddamn tourists stopped to take pictures of the bears.

Not planning forces me to take life as it comes, because it forces me into the present, to consider the sound and smell and light and heat. And when the left fork looks more interesting, I turn left.

I am getting used to the endless wind, slowing to 50 in crosswind gusts that sometimes knock me halfway across the lane. Luckily, there is little traffic on the secondary roads. When there is a tailwind, I speed up to 70 or more. In a tailwind I can hear the engine beating louder and feel the heat rising from the air-cooled cylinders.

Late in the day, canyons appeared like surprising gaps in the flat landscape. Mesas rose from the horizon. It felt as though the earth had been pressed up and down at the same time, making three levels, one higher and one other lower than the one I was skimming along.

Looking for a campground someone had suggested, I stopped to ask directions from a group of bicyclists gathered in front of a grocery store. Some of them were drinking from squeeze bottles, their heads tilted back to catch the stream of water. They wore colorful, tight-fitting spandex suits and short, ventilated helmets with chinstraps. Their bikes glittered with polished aluminum, some probably costing more than some motorcycles.

I rode up next to the group and raised my faceshield. Nobody turned in my direction. "Hey," I said. "Anybody know how to get to Caprock Canyons State Park?"

One of the bicyclists turned disdainfully toward me and said, "What? I can't hear you." The rest of the group ignored me.

"Do you know how to get to Caprock Canyons?"

He dismissed me by saying, "We're new here. Why don't you ask inside?" He turned back to the group.

The park turned out to be just down the road. The girl at the gate wanted to give me a primitive campsite, a one-mile pack-in with no facilities but really great scenery. I opted for the hot showers and flush toilets.

On my way back from dinner I saw the bicyclists at the campground. They had set up a group of high-tech tents around a red van. Most of them were lounging around, trying to maintain their attitude while the driver of their chase van prepared dinner.

The moon was full almost every night I spent on the Texas prairie. The night sky was clear and the blue light so intense it cast ghostly shadows.

I sat at the picnic table with my journal and let my mind shape whatever thoughts it wished. It reminded me of the many night watches I had spent at sea. Alert, waiting, and watching the cool light draw color and form from the blank sea and sky. I did not know it then, but I learned to respect my mind and to live comfortably with it on those long ocean nights.

Although I had never wished to be anywhere else, I wondered why I had ended up here. On a motorcycle. On the prairie. When I was at sea, I knew it was a natural place for me to be, a fulfillment of my childhood next to the ocean. But this place was foreign. A place I had never known as a child, only imagined, though I recognized a familiar quality. I remembered the line from my all-time favorite movie, *Lawrence of Arabia,* when Lawrence is asked why he likes the desert.

"Because it's clean," he replied.

Like the sea.

My father once told me that he rode across country on a motorcycle when he was at Harvard in the late 1930s. He said it took ten days. This was before I discovered his habit of reconstructing the past to suit his needs, like one remodels a house. Anyway, I was a kid and I believed him and the idea of this ride was born.

If I had not discovered my father's way of taking a dream and creating a myth so powerful that it seemed like the truth, I might not have taken this trip. I might have been content, like most people, to say, "someday." But fulfilling promises and realizing dreams has become an obsession for me.

So I sat in the moonlight on the prairie.

The next morning, I rode through the park before heading out. The canyons were what I saw as buttes as I rode in from the east. Approaching from the west, they would not be seen at all. That was the secret! I was on a big plate of earth, tilted slightly so that it cracked and rose from the once-level prairie. The wind and rain had eroded the ragged break into red, wild canyons and flat-topped mesas.

The level road out passed through dusty cattle country. The grass was almost white where it was seeding, but the overall landscape was yellow-green, as though I were looking through a filter. Occasional clumps of black trees on the horizon indicated ranch houses.

The sky was everything. It was like being at sea. Nothing but the sky and light that seemed to come from everywhere. Riding alone down the straight road was at once lonely and full, empty and complete, and I seemed to vibrate at a clear, high pitch. I tried to breathe in the bigness and my mind expanded to the horizon. I was the little dot at the center of a widening circle, the fixed point of a compass whose arc was the horizon and whose apex was the sky.

Heading toward the New Mexico border, the land changed to rolling waves before flattening out once more. I passed downwind of several huge feedlots and was stunned by the sour stench. At one of them, a steer stood on top of a large black mound of manure. Next to the pile was a backhoe. All the cattle were dirty with manure and stood sadly in the muddy pens with their heads almost touching the ground as though they were weeping in shame. It was an outrageously ugly scene of death and despair.

The smell stayed in my nostrils for a long time.

10

New Mexico

The KOA in Clovis, New Mexico, was conveniently located on the main street leading into this Air Force town. I parked in front and went in to register. When I came out there were two other Beemers parked next to mine. One was a beautiful metallic blue R100RT touring bike. Two women and a man, all wearing riding gear, were looking at my motorcycle.

"Hi," said the man. "Were you the guy that called me today?"

"No."

"Somebody called me out of the *Anonymous Book* and left a message on my answering machine. I was hoping it was you." The *Anonymous Book* contains a list of phone numbers of BMW Motorcycle Owners of America members offering assistance or hospitality to other members passing through their locality. I had not called so I said, "Sorry."

"Anyway," he said. "welcome to Clovis. Looks like you came a long way." He gestured at my New York license plate. "You want to go for a ride? We're going out to a place that has the best ice cream cones in New Mexico."

"I've been riding all day and I better take a break. The wind out here really wears me out."

"What wind?" he laughed. "Why, there's not enough to raise any dust at all. But is there anything we can do for you?"

"If you can suggest a good place to eat tonight, I would appreciate it."

"Sure, how about my place? We can barbecue some burgers and talk motorcycles. We'll go for our ride and stop on the way back for you. About two hours from now."

"I'd love it, but I don't want to impose."

"Hey, we don't get many Beemer riders through here. You're welcome. By the way, I'm Steve, this is Pat riding my old bike, and my daughter Faith."

While they were gone I set my tent up next to a Harley rider, unpacked, and showered.

Steve lived in a small subdivision house with a one-car garage jammed full of motorcycles. One of them was a mint 1974 Jawa 350cc two-stroke with a sidecar. Steve bought it with less than 2,000 miles on it. I had never ridden in a sidecar so Steve offered to take me out. It was an entirely different feeling racing along with your butt six inches off the ground. Half of the view was obstructed by the motorcycle on the left. In traffic, the cars towered over my head. I didn't like it as much as I expected. Too claustrophobic. It felt dangerous, although it was probably safer than a two-wheeler.

Steve bought his BMW the year before from a dealer in Albuquerque. He'd had the head ported and had installed lightweight wrist pins, dual plugs, and Mikuni carburetors—more than $1,800 in modifications. He said he had blown away a mildly hopped-up Harley in one of those classic midnight drag races. You know the kind.

Harley Owner to Steve: Why did you buy that piece of shit? It would have a hard time outrunning a donkey.

Steve: Oh yeah? Well, it will outrun that piece of shit you ride.

Harley Owner: Oh yeah?

And so on.

The Harley owner looked over Steve's bike after the race and noticed the dual plugs and Mikunis. "Hey," he said, "This bike ain't stock." He immediately tore down his bike and went very radical. Their second time out, the Harley blew up.

There are three forms of motorcycle fanaticism. Steve's buddies were cruisers, guys with attitudes and a love of chrome. I am a touring type, a traveling motorcycle cheapskate for whom distance is everything. And then there are the speed freaks, the guys in racing leathers you sometimes see on Sunday mornings bent over crotch rockets flying down deserted canyon roads.

Although Steve was a member of the BMW Motorcycle Owners of America (mostly touring types), there was no local chapter. So he spent a lot of his time with the local Harley club (cruisers). His girlfriend, Pat, was the club wiener bite champion, for which she earned the nickname "Fang." The wiener bite is an event at Harley rallies where women on the pillion take bites out of hot dogs suspended on strings as the rider goes by as slowly as possible. The winner is the woman who has the deepest throat. If this sounds a little obscene, it's supposed to.

We talked motorcycles most of the evening, but I did find out that Steve was a retired airman, which explained why he was in Clovis, which had a large air base. He was trying to get a computer consulting business going to help support his motorcycle obsession. He wanted to be able to go to BMW rallies and thought consulting would let him get free easier than a regular job. Of course, he thought full-time motorcycling would be ideal, but his pension was not enough to live like an ordinary poor person, much less a poor motorcycle fanatic.

Back at camp the next morning, I saw the Harley rider working on his machine and went over to see if I could help. "Problems?" I asked.

"The battery cap broke and acid is leaking all over," he said. The plastic cap had split in two. "I need to go to the Harley shop to get one of them, and some grease for the points. I changed the points yesterday but they didn't have any grease in the kit."

"You can use some duct tape to cover the hole until you get another cap," I said. I went back to my bike and got the roll of tape.

We had gained an hour when we crossed into another time zone at the New Mexico border and it was too early for a motorcycle shop to be open. Since we were both ready to go, I suggested we have breakfast together. Tom was a college student on his way to California to meet his father. He had inherited the Harley he was riding from his father, who had recently retired and was currently touring the West on a brand new Harley. Tom had worked two jobs last summer just so he could make this trip.

Tom wanted to get on the interstate to Albuquerque, so we decided to ride together until we crossed it. The feeling of being connected to somebody else on the same road was at once comforting and constricting. I felt less alone, but not as free.

I rode ahead for a while but Tom kept falling way back so I switched places and followed. It was good to see him ahead, a young college kid riding west on an old Harley piled with gear. He rode without gloves or helmet, in a black T-shirt he had bought in a Harley shop in Texas.

I felt old, with my full-face helmet, gloves, Levi's jacket, and electronic-ignition BMW. But Tom's face and hands were red and swollen from the wind and sun. His nose was covered with bits of flaking skin caked in the white ointment that he rubbed on every time we stopped. To tell the truth, he looked a little rough. I don't know if the image was worth the misery.

We stopped at Fort Sumner where Billy the Kid was killed, and paid $1 apiece to see a marker and a photograph showing the building where the shooting had taken place. Billy's grave was in a small cemetery behind a museum next to the state park. We went into the graveyard without going into the museum, having already paid once to see nothing. The grave itself was enclosed in a steel-barred cage to discourage vandalism. An outraged card on the cage said the headstone had been stolen once and recovered in California. They weren't taking any more chances.

We had lunch in a little place in Fort Sumner that served pinto beans and large dinner rolls that had been advertised as biscuits. Tom told me he was a political science major at Dickinson College. Like many college students, Tom was cynical about his future, recognizing that the secure lifestyle of his parents' generation was over.

"My Dad was just a factory worker, no college degree or any-thing, but he was making more than fifty grand a year. He worked at the same place all his life.

"I would be lucky to get a minimum wage job when I finish college. And there's no job security anymore. You can count on getting laid off before you get any seniority or start making good money. There's almost no chance my generation will do as well."

So this kid was on his way to see his father, who had lived the good life, riding his worn-out old machine.

Back on the road, Tom had a few problems. Another battery cap broke and Tom installed one of the spares he had gotten in Clovis. Then his bottle of sunblock came loose and I went back to get it. He also lost his sunglasses in a crosswind blast. I saw them shatter on the pavement. I gave him my spare set of sunglass straps. If this kept up, Tom wouldn't have much left when he got to California.

After Tom turned off, the road began climbing slowly into Santa Fe. It got noticeably cooler. The vegetation changed to small pine bushes dotting the hillsides.

I saw clouds with rain sheeting below, but nothing striking the dry ground. The cloudbursts were like separate disappointments, randomly starting and stopping in the distance. They put enough moisture in the air, however, to make a rainbow that was thick and colorful below the clouds, and thin and ghostly near the apex.

What I saw of Santa Fe the next morning was tourist-oriented, mostly boutiques, art galleries, and theme restaurants in adobe looking buildings. The downtown was clogged with cars and the road to Taos was lined with RVs and boat trailers. I wanted to see Taos, but not badly enough to endure the rush of pleasure seekers along the trashy highway that was in the midst of its transforma-tion into a service corridor of fast foods, gas stations, and home improvement centers.

I stepped off onto US 84. Smart move. I was soon in high plains country surrounded by mountains. It was refreshing after all the days of hot, windy, level highways. Like making port after a week at sea.

The road started its curving climb over the Continental Divide. Evergreen forest appeared, dark green against a sky that seemed to get bluer as I climbed higher, deepening from pastel on the horizon to cobalt at the dome. Even in the forest, there was a big, expansive feeling to the place, so open and full of potential that my heart ached.

It got steadily colder and I had to put on my leather jacket. The only other indication of the 11,000-foot altitude was the performance of the motorcycle, which had been laboring under load and was inclined to slow or stall at idle. Carbureted engines at high altitudes tend to run rich because there is no compensation for the reduced oxygen in the air. Luckily, by the time the problem got very bad, I was on the western slope where all the water that can make it that far drains into the Pacific Ocean. On the eastern side of the Divide, all the water drains into the Atlantic.

Back in the scrubby desert punctuated by mesas and odd rock forms, there seemed to be more motorcyclists on the road. I was passed by three biker types while I had been enjoying the view around a wide sweeping curve. The first rider was on a Yamaha Virago, a Harley-style V-Twin. He had a red bandanna around his head and wore mirrored aviator-style dark glasses. The second rider was on a Harley. The girl on the seat behind him nodded as they passed. They had a large duffel bag strapped on the back. The third was also on a Harley, one-up. None of the drivers had even glanced over at me.

I stopped for lunch at a small Mexican restaurant in one of the small towns that occasionally appeared and faded along the lonely road. Never more than a few blocks long, and only one story tall, the towns tried to minimize their vulnerability by huddling low and close together beneath the giant sky. Most were barely hanging on, the storefronts empty or occupied by flea markets, Salvation Army stores, and insurance agencies. There was usually a restaurant or bar or barbershop that still drew people, and the gas station and video store were always on the edge of town.

The menu had a number of dishes I had never encountered before. Curious, I asked the Hispanic waitress for help. Since I didn't want meat, she suggested I try the pozole with green sauce. "You'll like it, I promise."

It turned out to be something like hominy with a green sauce made of tomatillos. It was served with tortillas. Mexican food seemed to suit this countryside and I resolved to get as much of it as I could.

After lunch, while I was checking the map outside the restaurant, two motorcyclists on Japanese sport-touring machines came up to talk. They were older, probably retired businessmen, one of them from Los Angeles and the other from Colorado. Every year they met somewhere between their homes and rode together for a week or more.

Headed for Navajo Lake State Park, I took the indicated turn for the campground and ended up on a long dirt road leading to a boat ramp. There were a few campsites occupied by trailers, but there were no showers and it was far from anyplace I could eat. As I was turning around, I was startled by a passing truck and grabbed the front brake. The bike went down on its right side and the truck kept going. He probably never saw me.

The crash bars had prevented any damage to the engine cases, but I knew I couldn't get the bike up by myself. I had once tried to pick up another bike I had dropped and had only managed to push it over on the other side, screwing up both engine cases instead of only one.

I was angry and embarrassed at the same time. It was a dumb maneuver, the kind of mistake a beginner makes. I left the bike on the ground and went into the campground looking for help. I found a woman who said she would try to help and we went back out to the bike. A man in a pickup truck also stopped and the three of us had the bike up in seconds. It started right up. Unwilling to prolong my embarrassment, I thanked my helpers and rode quickly away, my ego hurting badly.

Because I needed to prove I could still ride, I decided to take the dirt shortcut along the lakeshore to the dam, saving myself 25 miles. As soon as I started I realized I had made another stupid mistake, but had no room to turn the bike around. A bruised ego can get you into all sorts of trouble.

The road was rutted, hilly, full of large stones, and curved along the shore of the artificial lake. I was actually lucky to be on a motorcycle, because even a jeep would have had trouble. I rode the inside rut, avoiding the washouts on the lakeside. Most of the time there was water below me on my left and the face of a steep cliff on my right. No guardrails.

Son-of-a-bitch.

After seven sweaty miles on the road, I came to the dam. There was a narrow one-lane road across the top, with a sheer drop on either side. Again, no guardrails. It was like riding a tightrope stretched across the canyon. Damn, I hate high places.

When I finally arrived, there was no attendant at the park. No showers here either, and by now I really needed one. This was turning into a bad day.

I rode back to the highway headed for a KOA campground in Bloomfield, missed the campground and ended up thirty miles farther down the road at a Motel 6. It was 7:00 and I had spent more than ten hours in the saddle.

I met a BMW rider at breakfast at a place that advertised "Meals for Working People." By now I was beginning to feel like one of the crowd and we fell easily into conversation, as though we had met before and preliminary positioning was not necessary. I told him I was trying to figure a way around the south of the Grand Canyon without going through Flagstaff. It looked like I would have to go a long way south on some dirt roads.

"No," he said. "Don't go that way. There's nothing out there off the main road. No gas stations, no towns, nothing. Just stay on this road and go through Flagstaff. It's not so bad."

I didn't have to decide until I got into Arizona so I headed out, once again foiling the planning monster.

Approaching Shiprock the mesas gave way to rolling desert dotted with large rocks that looked like South Pacific islands viewed from a small boat. Colonies of brown, flat-roofed buildings with rooftop swamp coolers clustered near the road like hornets' nests. Reservation housing. House trailers had been randomly placed as though they were still waiting to be arranged along the street. Abandoned cars with missing doors and front ends stripped to reveal greasy engines sat on blocks near the houses. There is no place to hide failures in this open landscape.

Beyond Shiprock the already sparse vegetation almost disappeared and the colors shifted from yellow to red. A dusty haze developed that deepened the colors. The road threaded through rock spires that resembled a gigantic mud castle made by a demon. Further on, gray domes, like huge oyster shells lying on a beach, dotted the landscape. The scale was immense and I felt shrunken, as though by becoming smaller I had made the place bigger. Unlike the prairie, which I found expansive, this place turned me inward, reminding me of my vulnerability and insignificance.

I have heard the desert described as timeless, but for me it seemed to be all about time. Millions of years of geology are on display on the desert, while we are lucky to survive eighty years. Our lives are only a blink here on the desert.

11

Halfway

I stopped for lunch at the trading post at Mexican Water, Arizona. Despite its seemingly remote location, the trading post was busy. It was the center of social and commercial activity for the region, and posters and handbills advertising potluck dinners, dances, used cars, and various personal services were displayed on a large bulletin board on the porch of the store.

Over lunch in the small, simple restaurant, I realized that I was halfway through my trip. Halfway is not a geographical place or a statistical observation. It is a state of mind, the point on a journey where one stops leaving and begins returning.

Up to now, I had been determined not to let go of The Ride. I struggled through the aching muscles and the doubts about my skills. I had to keep going, to prove to myself that I could do the thing that I had dreamed about for so long. Sure, I had been having the time of my life, but I also had been afraid I might not be able to go the distance. That worry had always been there in the background, pushing me along.

But here in this desert place, all these fears seemed to dissipate and I knew that I was going to make it the whole way. Over the hump. Halfway.

Climbing toward Flagstaff, the air, which didn't seem hazy before, became so transparent that objects in the distance seemed like scale models on a table before me. The desert reverted to grass similar to the western Texas prairie. Purple mountains grew on the horizon. It got cooler.

"Oh beautiful," I thought. "For spacious skies . . . "

"For purple mountains majesty . . . "

"America, America . . . "

My spirits always soared at these familiar words, but never as high as they did that moment.

The ride into Flagstaff was solitary except for a line of cars and motor homes at the entrance to the Grand Canyon. The campground on the way into Flagstaff was much larger and busier than any other KOA I had stayed in. I was assigned a tent site among some pine trees on a slope behind the campground. A group of French kids in a stretched passenger van drove in and set up tents that were stored on the roof of the van. They spoke excitedly in their lovely, musical language, probably about the sights they had seen that day. They were all wearing T-shirts from Western tourist attractions. I learned from the campground staff that camping tours were very popular with European students. It was an inexpensive way to see America.

After an uninspired dinner at the snack bar, I walked through the portable suburb of RVs back to the low rent area. A couple riding a Harley was setting up next to me. Chris and Christie, wearing Vietnam Veterans' colors, were from Tucson, Arizona. Christie was pissed. "These guys think because we ride motorcycles they can treat us like dirt. They put us way in back with no place to put up a tent. We paid just as much as anybody else."

"Hey, babe, it comes with the territory. This spot is better." When they saw their first campsite, Christie had insisted on going back and demanding something else. They had been assigned the first site because the campground people thought they would enjoy something private, meaning as far as possible from everybody else.

I wished I could have seen Christie demand her rights.

On my way to the bathroom to brush my teeth, I saw a Gold Wing parked next to a motorcycle camping trailer. It was a nifty setup, a tiny trailer that opened into a tent containing a full-sized bed and room to sit or change clothes.

Dwight and his wife Cindy, from Columbus, Ohio, were sitting on camp chairs in front of the trailer drinking beer.

"Did that couple on the Harley find a spot?" asked Dwight. "They went by a couple of times."

"Yeah, next to me."

"You're the guy on the BMW?"

"Yeah."

"How about a beer? It's nice and cold." Dwight reached back and opened the cooler strapped to the tongue of the trailer. There was a lantern and stove on the picnic table. A tarp protected everything from the sun. I sat down and we talked.

Dwight had retired after 20 years in the Army. He and his wife Cindy couldn't shake their wanderlust, so they toured on their Gold Wing every summer. They always set up as close to the bathroom as possible, because Cindy didn't like to walk far and besides, they met a lot more people since everybody had to use the bathroom. Except for the motor home people, who wouldn't talk to you anyway.

The next morning the air was cold and pine scented, and I joined the motorcyclists for breakfast at the outdoor concession stand. We were different people, but we lived with varying degrees of the same history and obsessions. Chris had never left Vietnam. The loud, powerful Harley-Davidson was his weapon. The leather vest with the Vietnam Veterans Motorcycle Club patch was his flak jacket. I understood. He had been drafted just out of high school with all the naturally violent tendencies of that age group, sent to a place where all moral restraint was suspended, and given a crazed kind of freedom to kill and destroy. The pumping mixture of fear, anger, and unrestrained violence was a tough high to come down from.

As a career soldier, Dwight did his time in Vietnam. But he was a pro. Yeah, Vietnam was like Korea, only hotter. Another war that you dealt with dispassionately, trying to make it to retirement. I understood. Survival. "365 days and a wake-up." Now he had bought the good life and was enjoying it.

I had volunteered. I was already on a ship off the coast of Vietnam, but we never encountered any Vietnamese. I guess I was getting bored and there was a good chance I would be reassigned to shore duty on my upcoming rotation, which would have been even more boring. And I had been immortal then, like everyone else under 30.

I never thought I would get the assignment. Combat zone shore billets were usually reserved for career officers, Regular Navy officers punching their ticket on the way to flag rank. I was just a Reserve officer, an OCS graduate. But I got it.

We had an easy, comfortable talk, like old friends meeting for breakfast, before heading off in our different directions.

The only road west out of Flagstaff is Interstate 40. It is a pretty route through the mountains. But the leveling of the roadway and the cuts through the crests of the hills created a bad wind-tunnel effect. I was glad to get off onto old Route 66, The Mother Road.

There were wonderful art deco style motels with signs that seemed to come right out of the Jazz Era. "If you don't stay here, we both will be sorry" and "Good Eats, Cheap." But most of the roadhouses and motels were in disrepair and some were boarded up. Too bad, it looked like it had been fun.

Then I broke out into a section of high green and yellow meadow. All alone. Just cruising. The road wandered around obstructions, dipped into valleys, and rose over hills. There was grass growing in the cracked asphalt. I had a feeling of connectedness with this road, a joyful feeling of travel altogether missing on the interstate. The sweet wind was light and steady.

A freight train overtook me and I waved at the engineer. He responded with two toots on his whistle. The freight cars rumbled along beside me for a while, then I was back in the quiet past.

I'd had a happy childhood, to compensate for the misery of my adolescence, I suppose. It was a warm, golden time, played out in an evergreen place full of safe things for kids to do. I walked barefoot everywhere, way up into Pauoa Valley where I could pick bananas at an abandoned plantation, or guava for my mother to make jam, or lilikoi to mix with orange juice, or mountain apples that were more like pears with red skins. I fished in Pauoa Stream for swordtails and rainbows, inch-long tropical fish that I trapped with a hand net and brought home to put in aquariums made of old gallon jars.

On Boat Days I went to the pier to watch the Lurline, Matsonia, or Mariposa passenger ships leave for the mainland. The passengers were up to their ears in flower leis that they would cast overboard as they passed Diamond Head, hoping the garlands would float ashore, insuring their return to Hawaii. When the ship's whistle blew the final signal, the passengers would throw streamers to their friends ashore, while the Royal Hawaiian Band, all dressed in white, played "Aloha Oe." The water under the stern of the ship stirred as it slowly eased away from the pier, the streamers stretching taut, then reluctantly breaking.

The tugboats hooted and I would run to see the boys swimming alongside the ship, diving for coins, sometimes dangerously close to the boiling water at the stern. I watched expectantly for some kid to be sucked into the propellers and be chopped to bits, but it never happened.

Afterward I would try to catch the little silvery fish that schooled under the pier, using a bamboo pole and a tiny hook on a two-pound leader. I bought a single shrimp for bait. I never caught anything but hope.

Sometimes old men would be crabbing along the breakwater, using nets tied to a stiff wire hoop. The nets were baited in the center with aku heads. The idea was to cast the net away from shore and wait until crabs tried to get the bait and entangled themselves in the netting.

I would walk along the breakwater looking into the crabbers' buckets and watching them retrieve the nets with a steady overhand pull, untangling the crabs, tossing the little ones back, arranging the cord, then casting the net with a wide sidehand sweep like a discus thrower.

Before I went home, I would stop in Chinatown and buy manapua for lunch, large, steamed buns filled with spiced meat, and I would wander through Chinatown eating and looking at displays of dripping fresh vegetables, and bright red and silver fish on mounds of melting ice. The sidewalks near them would be wet and cold on my bare feet. I perused the crack seed kept in rows of glass jars, buying a nickel's worth of my favorite, which was handed over in a tiny brown paper bag.

I would watch white-aproned butchers wield their wide-bladed cleavers, using only one knife to do everything from cutting chops to de-boning a fillet. Occasionally someone would buy a live chicken and I would watch while it was beheaded, bled, de-feathered, singed, and gutted. It was a quick, surgical operation and the buyer would be handed a package wrapped in pink butcher paper that was still warm to the touch.

Then I would head home, walking up Nuuanu Street past the Buddhist Temple where sometimes there were judo or sumo matches going on, or maybe preparations for a bon dance, past my cousin's house, and past the pastel green Square Deal Market on the corner of Pauoa Road.

It was like my experience so far on this journey. No, not the specifics. I mean seeing the world like a barefoot kid again. Experiencing the journey just as fully and completely through the widening cracks in my cynicism. Welcome back, kid, I knew I never grew up. I'll try harder from now on.

It got hotter and drier as I descended into the Mojave, the colors warming from alpine meadow to prairie to desert.

I stopped for lunch at a Chinese restaurant in Kingman, parking next to a rough-looking Harley with a large army issue duffel bungeed to the sissy bar. Once inside, it took a few seconds for my eyes to adjust to the dim light. The Harley rider was at the bar drinking beer.

I sat in a booth and ordered the Almond Chicken and Fried Rice Special for $2.95. It came with egg drop soup and a pot of tea. My fortune cookie said, "Good opportunities. Make up your mind to grasp the next." Not bad, since I was on my way to Las Vegas.

The Harley rider left the restaurant when I did. He was wearing Vietnam Veterans' colors and had a knife about a foot long hanging from his belt. He looked like he was still in the jungle.

"It's hot out here," I said, arranging my gear.

"Yeah," he said, nodding at my license plate. "Especially if you're not used to it."

"I'm not," I replied, surprised at his friendliness.

He started up and backed into the road as I was putting my helmet on. "Have a safe trip," he said as he rode away. "Be careful."

The seventy miles between Kingman and the Hoover Dam was the kind of desert I associated with the Sahara. Motorists were advised to keep their headlights on because the heat waves shimmering off the road surface could be worse than fog. It was hotter than I had ever experienced, the heat almost physical, like a heavy weight on my shoulders. There was no relief anywhere. No shade. Columns of dust rose, danced in the wind, then spiraled away. Sudden wind shifts, like currents in a boiling sea, pushed the bike around.

Halfway across, maybe because I knew it would be ending soon, I began to relax and enjoy the heat. I usually like the heat. I even had a sauna built in our basement at home and looked forward to sitting in it after a hard workout. The sweat cleans out the system.

I remembered my stint in Survival, Escape, and Evasion School before going to Vietnam. We had been confined in a mock prisoner-of-war camp where we were exposed to various interrogation and punishment techniques used by the north Vietnamese. I was put in a black corrugated iron box in the sun, after refusing to divulge any more than my name, rank, and serial number. It was hot and I must have been in the box for a half-hour. At first I worried about dying from dehydration, but I realized it would be hell to pay if any of the instructors killed anyone. So I reverted to my military survival plan, "Be patient, it will end soon."

It did. But not before I learned that I liked the heat. I liked the heat not because it was better than being cold, which I dislike, but because it felt good. Being in that box was not like lying on the beach in Hawaii, sweating out the poison of overindulgence while gathering the energy of the sun, but I got out just as clean and relaxed.

12

Las Vegas

On the way into Vegas there were billboards advertising CIR-CUS, CIRCUS, GUARANTEED ROOMS—$19.95. I stopped at an "Official Las Vegas Information Center" that turned out to be a tourist trap, pushing hotel rooms and casino show reservations.

A woman at the counter gave me a flimsy brochure with a map of the Strip showing the casinos. "I have a hotel room off the Strip for $30 a night and a casino right in the center of the Strip for $50."

Her voice was mechanical and I could tell she had already done this too many times today. "No $19.95 rooms."

I decided to ride to the Strip and see for myself.

The Strip, even in daylight, is impressive, an eye-searing white road lined with fantastic architecture representing everything from Ancient Egypt to the Pirate Coast. A row of gigantic hotels, each standing separately, each shouting its own outrageous statement. I laughed. This was beyond wretched excess, so extreme it was endearing. A fantasy world in the middle of the desert. A Mirage. An Oasis.

There seemed to be no doors at the entrance to Circus, Circus. Just a wide opening out of which flowed a current of cool air. It was like entering a cave full of glittering crystals. The casino was right there. Banks of slot machines jingled in the background. Long lines of people pushing luggage with their feet queued at the front desk.

I went to the hospitality desk and asked about a room. "Sorry, we're full, but take this to the motel across the street. They will give you the same price." She gave me a slip of paper. Wow. 3,000 rooms. Full.

The Algiers was a lucky break. It was a relic of old Las Vegas before it became a family vacation destination, a two-story pink stucco building surrounding a courtyard with a swimming pool in the center. My room was big, comfortably furnished, clean, and quiet, with none of the plastic tackiness of budget motels. I parked the motorcycle in the shade under the stairwell.

After a shower, I walked back across the wide street to Circus, Circus and through the door into the casino. There was no intervening lobby, no easy transition to the anxious frenzy of the casino. There seemed to be banks of slot machines everywhere. Women in mini-skirts carried trays of coins, making change, tucking folded bills between their fingers. The mechanical ringing of the machines and the multicolored lights flashing in the dim room made it seem like a factory floor.

People sat intently at the machines, their backs poised in anticipation. Behind the noise of the machines there was silence. Nobody spoke. Even winners, coins pumping out of their machines, were sober. No end zone dances, no high fives, not even an "All right!" Somehow, rejoicing seemed inappropriate.

I sat down at one of the bars scattered over the casino floor and ordered a beer. There was an electronic poker machine built into the counter in front of me that accepted $20 bills. A tray of pens was conveniently placed next to a plastic holder dispensing Keno cards. I watched a game of blackjack. The gamblers played almost mechanically, the dealer not even looking as he cleared or covered wagers. Eye contact seemed to be forbidden. This was serious stuff, a ritual of hope and disappointment played all alone. A lot like life, I guess.

Circus, Circus' attraction was a free circus act every half-hour. I decided to go because I was getting depressed sitting in the casino, even though the beer was inexpensive.

On the way out, I found a quarter sitting on a slot machine. I put it in and pulled the handle. Nothing. "Nuts," I thought, automatically putting my hand in my pocket for another quarter. Luckily, I didn't have any.

All the seats in the gallery were taken so I went to the mezzanine and leaned over the railing. There was a trapeze installed about two stories above the main floor. A safety net was stretched below. The ringmaster came out and introduced the act, two men and a woman performing a classic circus trapeze act. They were good, but it didn't seem like fun. There was listless applause when the show ended, and most of the audience stood up to leave before the ringmaster finished his description of the next show. There was a self-absorbed intensity in the place, and I walked off feeling dissatisfied and bored.

The floor I was currently on turned out to be the kids' area. There was an arcade featuring carnival games where the kids could win prizes. Classic ring toss, coin toss and sharpshooter booths dispensed plastic toys and stuffed animals to the winners.

I went into a large room full of sophisticated video games. One was an almost life-size motorcycle mounted on a platform in front of a four-foot high video screen. The idea was to race other motorcycles around a track. The controls all worked, although there was no shifting, and the bike could be leaned over for curves. I watched a kid crash several times as he jerked the handlebars in frustration. Even on an electronic motorcycle you have to use the controls smoothly.

The casino was getting tough to take, so I went to the $3.99 Buffet Dinner and stood in a long line of whining kids torturing numbed parents. It reminded me of Disney World. Every now and then a kid pushed too far and a parent flipped out, resulting in tears and a moment of embarrassed silence.

The buffet was like a school cafeteria for the children of the rich and famous. I pushed my tray along a shelf of stainless steel tubing. Past ten feet of salads. Tossed, three bean, pasta, cole slaw, Jell-O. Then ten feet of vegetables. Potatoes, rice, green beans, peas, and onions. Then ten feet of meat. Baked ham and pineapples, fried chicken, broiled haddock filets, tuna casserole. Then a man in a chef's hat carving from a large chunk of roast beef. By the time I got to the roast beef, I had covered my plate with food, so the chef simply placed the slice of meat on top. Desserts were at another table. A waitress served drinks.

Three double-sided buffet stations fed the continuous stream of people into the clamoring dining room. Someone who understood queuing theory had worked out the traffic flow carefully, and I was able to find an empty table quickly. I sat down, marveling at the efficiency with which the 3,000 rooms of people were fed. Wow. And it was pretty good food too.

"Do you mind if we join you?" A young couple stood at the table.

"Not at all," I said, glad for some company.

They put their trays down. "It's incredibly crowded and there don't seem to be any free tables." She had a clipped British accent that made her sound much older than her appearance.

"I can't believe this place," said the young man. "So American!"

"And so inexpensive! I can't believe this meal only cost $3.99. And our hotel is only $25. Incredible!"

"The gamblers pay for all this," I said. "As long as you don't gamble, Las Vegas is the cheapest first-class vacation in the world. But if you gamble, it could be the most expensive."

They introduced themselves as Lucy and Oliver, two friends just out of high school in England. Oliver had finished the year before and was about to start University in the fall after a year of work and travel around Europe. Lucy just finished high school and was also starting University in the fall. They were just friends, both having other romantic engagements.

They had Greyhound Bus passes which allowed them to travel anywhere in the country for a month. They had already been to Washington, Iowa, and Montana. Sometimes they stayed with host families. Otherwise, they traveled at night, sleeping on the bus and spending the days exploring the little towns that interested them. They tried to avoid the big cities, which they thought might be expensive and dangerous. They were headed to Texas and Florida next.

Las Vegas was an unexpected stop for them. When they arrived, instead of transferring to another bus, they decided to visit the Strip. "Once we were here, we knew we had to stay over."

Oliver was keeping a diary and had written more than 100 pages so far. Lucy took lots of pictures but preferred to sketch. They were so full of youthful enthusiasm and curiosity that it made me happy to be with them.

After dinner we walked down the strip to the Flamingo. The sidewalks around the entrance were crowded with people. Suddenly, there was a hissing that rose to a loud roar. Fountains of water illuminated by red and yellow lights shot from the top of the volcano. We were right on time for the half-hourly eruption. It was all done with lights and water and sound effects and was so artificial that it seemed hardly worth the effort. But, caught up in the instant fantasy, we laughed and cheered with the crowd.

My motel was on the way back so they stopped to look at the motorcycle. Oliver took my picture with it. Then we said good night and retreated to our rooms.

I took the next day off, lounging by the pool and writing in my journal.

The hotel clerk, a large man with a salt-and-pepper mustache, said it was 105 degrees, not too bad for the middle of summer. I was anticipating my trip across Death Valley and decided I had to leave by 5:00 a.m. to get across before the heat really set in. I asked the desk clerk if the office would be open that early. He said "Don't worry, there'll be somebody here. Vegas never closes."

He was right. 5:00 a.m. could have been any other hour in the neon darkness. I saw a guy crossing the street with a beer in his hand. There was a white Rolls Royce limo waiting in front of the Wedding Chapel.

Passing through the honky-tonk downtown at the north end of the Strip, mini-skirted night ladies waited patiently on corners. The downtown had a dark edge that was hidden by the glitter of the Strip. Here it was easy to imagine men with slicked back dark hair and pencil-thin mustaches, sitting at green felt card tables, drinking whiskey. On the Strip, everyone wore Bermuda shorts.

13

Death Valley

I had breakfast at a truck stop on the civilian north side of Las Vegas. A trucker, his face and hands seared from years in the desert sun, sat next to me at the counter. His skin was stretched thin across his cheeks and was deeply wrinkled everywhere else. When I told him I was going to Death Valley, he said, "I wouldn't go in there with a motorcycle."

Shortly before 9:00 I turned left at Beatty, headed for Daylight Pass in the Funeral Mountains. Signs on the road advised motorists to proceed at their own risk, carry water, and insure their vehicle was in good working order. I was alone on the warming road.

This approach to Death Valley drops from 5,000 feet above sea level, to 300 feet below sea level. The valley shimmered like a smoldering fire pit. A smoky yellow haze obscured the details. The landscape around me was searing. Black rocks lay in red soil like fresh coals in a blast furnace. As I followed the winding road down, I could feel the temperature increase steadily, like easing slowly into a hot bath. I was gleefully happy, finally arriving at this fiery place, and I shouted wild, crazy things at the rocks.

I stopped at turnouts and watched the shadows disappear under the rising sun, whitening the valley floor. There were water tanks with warnings not to drink from them. The water was for overheated automobile engines.

The floor of the valley looked like it had been burnt by a flame-thrower. The temperature at the ranger station was 110 degrees. It would go over 120 this afternoon. I stayed long enough to drink a bottle of chilled spring water in the narrowing shade of the ranger station. Behind the ranger station there was a large, empty, parking lot.

Coming out through the mountains, the narrow road climbed steadily without guardrails. I turned off into an old mining town beside what first appeared to be a lake, but turned out to be bluish sand. The town claimed to have a population of 50, but at one time it had been much bigger.

Almost all the houses were abandoned, with ripped screens and broken windows. Old cars, bleached and drying, sat in dusty yards. I drove down several blocks and saw only one occupied house. An old man working on a faded red truck looked up surprised as I rode by.

I stopped at the California Information Center to ask directions to Manzanar, one of the Japanese Internment Camps during the Second World War. In the hysteria following the attack on Pearl Harbor, Japanese-Americans on the mainland had been rounded up and placed in what amounted to prisoner-of-war camps. This did not happen in Hawaii, not only because of the impracticality of interring more than a quarter of the population, but also because Hawaii's economy would have been crippled, doing more damage than the Japanese bombers.

Before the war, my grandmother, like other first-generation Japanese women in Hawaii, had worn kimono. When she learned the Japanese had attacked Pearl Harbor, she burned all her kimono in the back yard. After Pearl Harbor, kimono were no longer seen on the streets of Honolulu and old Japanese women wore simple, dark dresses like their southern European counterparts.

Because young, Japanese-American men from Hawaii were eager to prove their loyalty, the 442nd All-Nisei Regimental Combat Team was formed. The 442nd was the most decorated unit in the war and it incurred the most casualties. Today, almost every Hawaiian-born Japanese family has a relative who served with the 442nd.

The internment experience created a different society of Japanese-Americans on the mainland. Hawaiian-born Japanese were much more comfortable with their American identity and blended easily into the Hawaiian melting pot. Mainland Japanese, however, became an aloof and distrustful ethnic minority. Their imprisonment turned them inward, to ancient ceremonies and customs, for comfort and support.

Occasionally, mainland relatives would visit Hawaii. We never understood them. They were so Japanese, so formal and polite, like our grandparents. We called them "Kotonks," after the sound of the hollow wood drum that is heard in Japanese ceremonies or the sound of knocking on a wooden dummy's head.

So I went to Manzanar curious to see a place that had so drastically altered the lives of my fellow Japanese-Americans, but had left me untouched. It was just up the highway.

Except for a stone gate, it was indistinguishable from the rest of the dry, scruffy, valley floor. The gate was substantial, having been built by the prisoners out of rock collected in the area. A stone guardhouse stood in the center of the wide entry. There were no other buildings left. A sign on the guardhouse indicated that Manzanar was a National Historic Site managed by the National Park Service. I had gotten here just in time, because there were plans to develop it into a real park with interpretive walks and clean restrooms.

I walked into the camp, looking at the foundations of the old buildings and the circular stone wall surrounding what was once a decorative garden. Scratched into the concrete were the Japanese names of the builders of the garden. Now it was only dust and weeds.

I found an unmaintained road leading through the camp and rode the motorcycle back to the old graveyard surrounded by a barbed-wire fence. In the center of the graveyard was a large white stone in the shape of an obelisk. The column was inscribed with black Japanese characters. People had left flowers, now dried to yellow memories, and small Buddhist offerings on the base of the monument. An incense pot. Red origami cranes. A few black pebbles.

The white stone gleamed against the blue mountains enclosing the valley. It could have been a lovely setting except for history. Except for the dusty foundations on the other side of the barbed-wire fence.

14

California

I continued up the Inyo Valley in the afternoon shadow of the Sierras. Elaborate irrigation systems fed the crops. The hills were dry but in the valleys were rich seams of emerald and jade.

I began to feel the pressure of too many people in a place meant to be dry and lonely. Food was more expensive, even in the very modest places that I usually looked for. There were lots of elaborate motor homes on the road and parked in scenic overlooks. Parking lots had oversize spaces just for them.

The campground listed in the guidebook was a dusty parking lot for RVs. I decided to keep going and found a pleasant, grassy campground in the next town. A group of students traveling in a pair of vans was camped in the center of the tenting area. They were preparing dinner as I set up. It was a well-orchestrated group effort, with people assigned to washing vegetables, cooking, and setting the tables. Their group leader gave crisp instructions in German.

I went to dinner at a small Mexican restaurant that was inundated by French students as I was halfway through my meal. I tried to help the owner explain the menu, but the cultural gap was too wide to bridge with our limited understanding of each other's languages. I didn't know enough French and Spanish, the owner didn't know enough French and English, and the students didn't know enough English and Spanish.

On my way out of the campground, a man asked, "Did you ride that bike all the way from New York?"

"All the way."

"I ride an enduro myself. Mostly down in Mexico where there's more dirt roads and less hassles with the environmentalists."

I didn't want to pick up that stone, so I started the engine. "Sounds like fun."

"Yeah. Well, see you later."

At breakfast a BMW rider came over. "Is that your GS outside?"

"Yeah."

"You're a long way from home. I ride an RS." Like all other areas of human interest, there is an insider's language among BMW enthusiasts that allows us to instantly establish our position. For example, he now knows I am a serious long-distance rider on a machine designed for third-world touring. And I know he is a purist, an air-cooled fanatic on a unique sporting machine. We can talk.

"I'm trying to avoid the four-lane road to Mono Lake," I said. "How is Old Route 6?"

"That will be slow going. The four-lane is a nice ride. Beautiful scenery."

"Okay."

The four-lane road turned out to be clogged with big RVs and angry automobile drivers trying to pass. I turned off onto Old Route 6 and was instantly back into country. I rode alone up a wide valley to a small town with an old general store. There were old horse drawn wagons nodding in the yard along with rusting farm tools and big-wheeled tractors.

The road climbed to Deadman Summit above Mono Lake. Happy whoops dropped down out of sight before bouncing up over the next ridge. Killjoy modern highway builders would have blasted through them. The 8,000-foot summit was cold and the light was intensely blue and clean. On the way down there was a scented redwood forest like a refreshing sweet after a pleasant meal. The view of Mono Lake must have been better than any along the four-lane highway.

North of Mono Lake the highway reverted to two-lanes and the traffic slowed to the least common denominator, the dreaded RV. Yosemite traffic headed for Lake Tahoe. I didn't mind the slower pace because the ride was pretty, snaking along some clear trout streams, but there was a frustrated urgency in the line of cars that seemed to infect everything. Finally, I stopped and watched a fly fisherman casting in a small pool, almost up to his waist in the water. It was better after that.

There were many motorcycles on the road and I seemed to be waving all the time. I started out raising my hand in greeting. But after a while I just let go the handlebar with my left hand and gave them a cool five, my arm straight out and low.

My strategy was to stay well inland to avoid the congestion, then cut over to the coast north of San Francisco. That meant I had to go back into Nevada and through Reno, across the point where California's eastern border kinks.

Reno had a vague Times Square feel to it. Lots of lights and tall buildings overshadowing the street. Hustlers and suckers both looking for gold on the sidewalks. It was an older, rougher town with none of the Disney feel of Las Vegas. It figures. Reno is the divorce capital of the world. This is where the fantasy ends, not where it begins.

The afternoon ride was an ordeal. I had to do a long freeway stretch followed by a lights-on-in-daylight section because of the sudden dust storms. Cool air draining from the Sierras made rivers of strong winds that pushed the bike around. I had to wrestle with it just to stay in my lane. I decided to stop at the Super Budget Motel on the way into town. Except for a few cars, the parking lot was empty. I walked into the lobby, taking off my helmet. As I approached, the woman at the front desk nervously rearranged the penholder and registration pad on the counter. I guess I looked like an outlaw biker to her.

I had not encountered this kind of reaction before and played it for everything I could. "How about a room?" I said, putting my helmet on the counter.

"We're kind of full," she replied, hoping I would be discouraged.

"How full?"

"Almost."

"Well, give me a room."

A man wearing a dress shirt and tie stepped behind her. "All I have are way in back," she said.

"I want to be near the bike."

The woman looked very nervous and fiddled with a stack of blank registration cards. The dress shirt and tie stepped up to the counter and said, "Why don't you give him 11. He can park right in front."

Too bad. I was starting to get pissed off and had been looking forward to dumping on the stupid broad. Of course, shitting on her would have simply reinforced her prejudice against motorcyclists. That's how prejudice works, start it going and it feeds on itself.

I detected a subtle change in attitude as I crossed into California. Little kids no longer came over to ask questions. Instead, they stood at a distance and looked, as though constrained by an invisible leash. Owners of RVs parked at scenic pullouts and ate their lunch inside, taking in the view through picture windows. Solitary fishermen sorted dry flies. Motorcyclists waved to each other. When I stopped for film in a camera shop, the clerk said, "You are going to Manzanar." People suggested Chinese restaurants whenever I asked about a place to eat, as though everyone was supposed to travel in their own dimension. RVs. Fishermen. European students. Motorcyclists. Asian-Americans.

I had started the day riding with my leather jacket but the elevation soon required more. I stopped at an abandoned motel next to a bright green mountain meadow surrounded by dark pines, to change gloves and put on a sweater. The road through Lassen Volcanic National Park was narrow and wound through a high pass. There were no guardrails. Defiant pines grew between meadows of black volcanic ash. The sky was absolutely blue. A landscape painted in three colors. Simple. Clean.

Descending into Redding, the air warmed and I had to stop several times to shed layers. I was back in desert clothing by lunch. The next pass was only 3,000 feet, but it was even colder than Lassen and I had to change back to leather and a sweater. The downhill side faced the Pacific Ocean and over the crest the air suddenly thickened and could be felt in the lungs. The ocean wind clouded overhead and dumped rain on the windward slope, making a lush and damp forest sweet with pine and memories of the sea.

Unfortunately, I was on a busy scenic route that was also used by logging trucks. Automobiles, motor homes, and logging trucks careened down the winding road in a frenzied rush to the ocean. There were no places to turn off, and what could have been a pleasant ride soon turned into a damp ordeal.

I hit US 101 just north of Eureka and joined a stream of RVs, all of us headed north looking for a place to camp. The first place I tried was full. The next had no showers or other amenities. Also full.

I rode through the camping area again to be sure I had not missed a potential site. On the way out, a young blond man ran out and flagged me down.

"Are you looking for a campsite?" he asked in a heavy German accent.

"Yes," I said.

"It's full, but you can share my campsite. There is room."

He saved my ass. I was getting pretty tired and discouraged by that time, and was developing a burning hatred of motor homes.

Franz was a university student on holiday. He was riding a Yamaha enduro outfitted with aluminum panniers. The license plate was German. His motorcycle looked a lot like mine, except smaller. He said he was very excited when he saw me ride by on the BMW. It was his dream motorcycle. "Someday, I will own one of them," he said.

While I set up my tent, he explained that it was cheaper to bring his motorcycle from Germany than to rent one in the U.S. He considered buying a motorcycle here and taking it back to Germany, but the taxes made this option prohibitive. He could have tried to sell the bike before leaving, but negotiating the purchase and sale, in addition to getting the bike insured and registered, would have consumed his entire vacation. It may not have been possible anyway, since he was not a resident.

Before I went to dinner, I walked to the beach. There was a sand dune barrier blocking the view. Behind the white wall I could see the triangular tops of sails belonging to a flotilla of colorful Hobie Cats. In the glittering, late afternoon calm, I was happy that the sun would soon be setting, as it always did in my memory, over the sea. Two months ago I had turned my back on a gray Atlantic beach and started to come here. It had been an indirect and often uncertain approach, as I suppose all such trips must be. But I had made it.

How did I feel? Okay. Tired from the day's ride, but okay. I wasn't elated. I didn't feel like running down to the water and putting my toe in. I felt more like I had just finished a wonderful meal. Satisfied.

I went out to dinner and when I returned, the young couple next to us asked us over for a cup of coffee. They were living in Seattle but had quit their jobs and were traveling for a few months before settling in Colorado. Mike was an engineer. His hair was cut short and he had an efficient, plastic pocket-protector manner. Stacy was small and also had a short, no-nonsense hairdo. She had an earnest, middle-class style that her rugged outdoor clothing could not disguise. They surprised me. I would have expected a couple like this to be sitting in their starter home watching their favorite sitcom, instead of sitting at a picnic table with a couple of scruffy motorcyclists.

The sun was beginning to set and the sky overhead was darkening. There was a bright line along the top of the darkening barrier sand dune.

"We had good jobs," said Mike. "I was working at Boeing and Stacy was a medical secretary at a big clinic. We figured if we were going to do anything, we had to do it soon, before we got too settled."

"Plus, we want to live in Colorado," said Stacy. "It rains too much in Seattle."

"So we quit our jobs and got rid of all our stuff except for what's in the truck. We want to visit some of the national parks and make a loop into Texas before going to Colorado."

"Do you have jobs in Colorado?"

"Not yet, but we should be able to find something. I went to college in Boulder."

"I think what you are doing is great," I said. "But aren't you worried?"

"Our parents are worried. But we needed to do this. We always did everything that was expected of us. We worked hard in high school and stayed out of trouble. We went to college. We got good jobs. We got married . . . "

"But we never had any fun. We weren't, you know, free . . . "

"No, we had fun. But it was always, like, there was something more we were missing . . . "

The light had a misty yellow tint and the bright line above the barrier dune was orange.

"I know," said Franz. "I felt like that when I finished high school. So I took my motorbike to North Africa and rode around all summer before I started University. Now I am starting my last year of University, so I came to the United States. Maybe when I finish University it is over for a while."

"I think young Europeans travel much more than Americans. They are more curious about other cultures . . . "

"What about you, Notch? Why are you out here?"

"I guess I'm chasing dreams like you are. They never end. Each adventure just seems to up the ante. You just keep wanting to do more. And the desire, the restlessness, gets worse.

"You kids are in for interesting lives. I guarantee that. Once you start traveling like this, you will never want to stop. You'll never be content with a guided tour again. You won't be able to ride in an air-conditioned bus and take the same picture that mil-lions of tourists before you have taken."

The sky was peach-colored near the horizon and faded to burnt orange overhead.

"The best kind of travel is hard. I mean, it should be open to everything. To the weather, the rain and cold, the sun and heat. To the place, the rocks and water and trees. To the people, to their stupidity and their wisdom. Look, you can spend your life hiding, trying to be comfortable and secure, or you can go out and enjoy it."

The purple evening spread west and it was soon dark. Dark-ness by the sea is like being covered by black velvet.

"You will never be as free as you are now. Everything you own you can carry with you. I have to go a long way from home to begin feeling free. And even then there's the house and yard and cars to go back to. Sometimes I wish I could just stay out here, on the road."

We talked till late, recounting our adventures and finding sim-ilarities in everything we did.

15

The West Coast

The next morning I left before anybody else was awake. I stopped at the Shoreline Market for breakfast. There were two motorcycles and a tractor-trailer parked in front. I walked in carrying my helmet and one of the motorcycle riders asked me to join them at a large table. The two truckers on the rig outside were also at the table. There was nobody else in the restaurant.

We talked about travel. The truckers spent all but two weeks of the year on the road, and had been doing it for years. They slept in the rig, alternating driving to keep moving, and stopping in truck stops to shower and refuel. Both of them were divorced. "It comes with the territory."

They both agreed that trucking was a tough way to make a living, but they didn't think they could do anything else. Whenever they were not on the road they usually got drunk, holed up with some woman, and regretted it later. The road imposed a discipline they knew they needed to survive.

The two bikers were traveling together on a five-day vacation trip up the coast. They stayed in motels because they found the campgrounds were usually crowded and had lousy facilities, as I had discovered.

I brushed my teeth and shaved in the men's room before heading out.

The morning ride was cold and damp. There was a steady drizzle and occasional patches of fog. The colors were green and gray, glowing in the hazy light.

The road occupied me as I negotiated the curves, the motor homes, and the other motorists. But on clear sections, my mind drifted away to human contacts, last night's conversation, old friends, regrets. Rainy day thoughts.

US 101 must be one of the most beautiful highways in the country. Black cliffs dropping to the sea are followed by sandy beaches. Then coves that ache for a sailboat at anchor. Glassy lagoons. Chalk lines of surf. The setting was magnificent, but the road was a frustrating ordeal of laboring motor homes creeping around curves designed for passenger cars. Hills were especially slow going because the long rear overhang and long wheelbase of the motor homes could get hung up in the dips and crests. This road wanted to be ridden hard, but all I could do was idle along behind.

There seemed to be hundreds of motor homes on the road, but it felt lonely. They were inside and I was out. It was like walking through a suburban neighborhood on a rainy afternoon.

On the way into the restaurant for lunch, I stopped to admire two mint 1957 and 1958 Corvettes. Parked nearby was a Lotus Elan covered with rally decals and sponsor logos.

There were lots of expensive cars on the road. Yesterday I watched a couple taking pictures of an early Jaguar roadster parked by the side of the road. The woman was wearing a green wool dress and a long white scarf. The man had on a tweed riding jacket and a matching cap. The car looked brand new, although it must have been forty years old, at least.

There were unusual motorcycles as well. At a gas station I saw a red, white, and blue Honda CX500 Turbo, an insanely fast machine. The rider was wearing matching red, white, and blue leathers. His eyes were rubbed red and he had the crazed look of a true fanatic. He was riding with a guy on a red metallic Honda Hurricane who shook his head and looked skyward as they pulled out. I could hear the Turbo howling for a long time.

I was astounded by the extent to which people around here pursued their transportation obsessions. Expensive motor homes, rare automobiles, and exotic motorcycles. Not just a few, either, but hundreds. People wore their vehicles like T-shirts proclaiming their identity.

There is too much money out here, I thought. But what I meant was, I don't have enough.

I thought back over the day as I lay in my sleeping bag on the soft ground. Although the ride had been beautiful, I couldn't respond to it. Instead, I kept thinking about everything people had. I felt vaguely unsatisfied. Like realizing I was hungry after being fully absorbed in something else.

I saw a perfectly restored MG TF1500 identical to one I used to own, painted the same orange-red. "Wow," I thought. "I would love to have one of them again!" I always think the same thing when I see a T-series MG.

I saw several BMW 2002s with round taillights that looked as if they had just rolled off the showroom floor. I wondered what one would cost out here, having been fitfully searching for just such a treasure in rust country.

I saw a red 1967 Mustang like one I bought when I got back from Vietnam. And the aqua 1957 Thunderbird that I lusted for when I was in high school.

Do this all day and, sooner or later, the wanting begins. Desire is an insidious thing. It felt like I had gone into a fancy department store only to discover that there were a lot more things I needed besides the Jockey underwear on sale that week.

I knew that to see without desire is the key to happiness. This practice doesn't help the GNP, but it was one of the things I was working on. Clearly, I had a way to go, and the West Coast presented a unique challenge.

It rained overnight. I packed the tent wet and got on the road early. I wanted to cover the 340 miles to my layover in Olympia, Washington, in one day. It would be a long day, but I had had enough of the West Coast and was anxious to get it over with.

The road was dry when I left, but by mid-morning it began to rain again. Logging trucks left a pine-scented wake that floated in the air long after they were gone. Further north the parade of fancy vehicles thinned out but I was never on the road alone.

The only restaurant I could find for lunch was an expensive seafood place with white linen tablecloths and napkins. Stemware water goblets. Bread plates. Pats of butter preserved on crushed ice. And a dinner plate at each place that the waiter whisked away when he delivered the main course. I ordered a fish sandwich and felt uncomfortable, as though I didn't belong there. Somewhere back on the road, I had become a poor man. And now I understood what "exclusive" meant.

Like a flashback to the '60s, I saw skinny, bearded men in blue jeans and olive-drab Army jackets thumbing rides along the road. They sat on battered backpacks holding hand-lettered signs. Most were headed south into the eye of Hurricane Materialism. Tough going, too, since the RVs and collector cars on the road weren't inclined to stop for them.

After crossing the state line into Washington, I rode off the Coast Highway to Leadbetter Point at the end of a peninsula enclosing Willapa Bay. It was a relief to be finally alone on the road again and I could suddenly feel the sea like a blue surge. The salt sense scoured my mind clean and I was back in The Ride. I loved the austerity of these lonely roads. This was the only way I could become free. Reducing life to its simplest terms. Moving from place to place. Rootless. No attachments. Few needs and wants.

Part 3
Alaska

16

Olympia

When I was in high school, my cousin Janice married a big, happy sailor named Raz. His voice matched his name, sounding like a file shaping sheet metal, a voice created by too many cigarettes and late nights in smoky bars. He had blond hair worn in a short military haircut and his red face blended into his pink scalp. Everyone instantly liked him.

I couldn't imagine Janice married to anyone else. She had a defiant posture, which gave her a tough-girl look, but she had a loose, irreverent style that matched Raz perfectly. They had a lot of laughs together.

Janice's mother, my Auntie Kiyota, lived with them. She was part of the deal. It saved money and she kept Janice company during Raz' long cruises to the North Pacific. Auntie looked like one of the tiny old widows that one expects to see at afternoon mass in churches in Italy. She retired with a good pension after cooking in a school cafeteria for more than 20 years. It was hot, demanding work, but she was proud of what she had achieved.

Raz called Auntie "Bubbles," which caused her to huff and exclaim, "You're so disrespectful!" But she always smiled because she enjoyed the attention.

Things weren't perfect, however.

Raz is an alcoholic. A binge alcoholic, the worst kind. One of those people whose first drink launches a process that soars high then lands out-of-bounds like a foul ball. It is a common form of alcoholism among sailors. A month at sea then a few days of liberty. Just enough time to have a few drinks, get the tattoo touched up, and visit the massage parlor. "Hey, do you think that babe is still at the Black Cat? You know, the one with the big tits?"

That's how it starts. It usually ends in some whorehouse or after-hours sleaze joint being pumped for your last buck. Most of the men gave up when they ran out of money or retained enough sense to get back to the ship before their liberty expired. The serious drunks pawned their valuables and kept going until they passed out. If they were lucky, they would get picked up by the shore patrol and delivered to their ship before it got underway. Or their shipmates went out looking for them.

The drunks were usually happy, friendly guys, good at whatever they did aboard ship. So we laughed at them as they suffered through the first few days at sea. Then we forgot about it until the next time we were in port.

There were some desperate times for Janice when Raz disappeared for days, then had to get straightened out for his cruise. But she insisted that he was a good sailor. "When he went aboard ship he was sober and sharp. There were times I wished the damn ship would stay out at sea so he wouldn't get drunk."

Raz had been a classic.

Then he straightened himself out. He joined AA and started going to weekly meetings. He has been sober for more than 20 years, but he is still an alcoholic, no longer yearning for a drink, but fully aware that just one will put him back on the path to hell.

They tried to make it in Hawaii for a few years after Raz retired from the Coast Guard, but Hawaii is expensive and Raz couldn't find work that was not humiliating after so many years as a petty officer. So they chose a modestly comfortable retirement in Olympia, Washington, over the slow drip of advancing poverty in Hawaii. Olympia is an unpretentious town, the state capital of Washington, but better known as the home of Olympia Beer. There is a large Sea Services presence in the area and there were military recreational facilities, medical help, and PXs nearby. It worked for them.

They lived in a neighborhood of almost identical bungalows that had been personalized by their owners over the years. Their house was easy to pick out because the yard had been planted by someone used to tropical profusion. There were flowers planted everywhere, in neatly tended plots.

Raz walked out of the garage as I rode up the driveway. He had gained a lot of weight and moved like a fat man, pushing his belly ahead of him as though he were maneuvering a wheelbarrow. He was wearing a plaid shirt that bulged between the buttons, and he peered at me through thick, plastic-rimmed, military-issue glasses, the evidence of a Cold War wound inflicted by staring too long at radar screens trying to pick out Soviet missiles. He never got a Purple Heart.

"Hey, Notch," he said, his familiar voice rasping a Hawaiian-style greeting. "Howzit, bruddah?"

"Hey, Raz," I automatically responded. "Looking good."

But I was concerned. Raz' face seemed puffy and flushed. A fold of fat encircled his neck and his chin nestled in it as though it was a pillow. He seemed winded by the minor effort of walking out to see me.

I shut off the motor and put the bike on the kickstand.

Janice came out of the house laughing. "Hey," she said, "You made it. Son-of-a-bitch. You really rode that thing all the way out here."

Margaret followed Janice out the door. She had arrived earlier in the day and was already comfortably settled. "Hi, Notch," she said, as though I had just come back from a Sunday ride. "How was the ride?"

I relaxed into the easy, comfortable hospitality that I grew up with. Hawaiians call it the "Aloha Spirit," a way of accepting people just as they are—including ourselves. I felt it here and almost everywhere I had been on the back roads of the heartland.

We went into the house to say hello to Auntie. She was sitting in a large overstuffed chair that made her seem much smaller than I remembered. She had shrunk over the last few years, as though she was exhausting her physical presence in the last days of her life.

"You finally made it," she exclaimed. "We were getting worried about you."

Old people in Hawaii, and everywhere else, I suppose, never seem to waste much time on greetings. I felt as though I had come in from another room, and we were about to resume a conversation we had interrupted a few minutes ago, as though I had never left her mind in the five years since we last spoke.

"I had to cover a lot of ground today, Auntie."

"You know, you shouldn't ride that motorcycle so much. It's dangerous."

"Come on, Ma," said Janice, "Notch knows how to ride. He made it all the way across the country without any problems."

"Well, it's dangerous, and you know it."

"So, Auntie, how are you doing?" I asked, trying to head off a discussion about motorcycle safety.

"Oh, getting old. You don't want to get old. It's no fun."

"Being old and stubborn is worse," said Raz. "She fell down in the garden last week and lay there for a couple of hours without calling for help. Lucky thing I had to get something in the back yard. Otherwise she would have been out there until suppertime."

Clearly, Auntie was not taking the aging process gracefully. She was too proud and independent.

"Ma goes to the Senior Citizens' Center a couple of times a week," said Janice.

"Oh, that place is terrible," said Auntie. "It's full of old farts."

"We're trying to get Ma married off," said Raz. "But it ain't working. It must be her personality."

"Why do you think I want to marry some old fart at the Senior Citizens'?" said Auntie, acting indignant at the idea.

"Yeah, none of them can get it up anymore," laughed Raz.

"Look who's talking," said Janice, laughing even harder.

In Hawaii, we call this kind of easy conversation, "talk story." It's what happens whenever people meet without an agenda. It is possible people talk story more in laid-back, tropical places, but I have been talking story all the way across this country in the same way I might have been if I had been sitting with my friends at Ala Moana Park.

In restaurants, around campfires and picnic tables, people have shared their experiences, enriching me in the process. We solved most of the world's problems and designed the world's best touring motorcycle. We planned dream trips that will resonate in our minds until we finally break out and go. We worried about beef prices (too low) and gasoline prices (too high). We talked story.

It was dinner before I got a chance to ask about Raz. He had joined a support group to quit smoking but was having trouble controlling his weight. "But," he said, "the doctor said it is better to be fat than dead. Anyway, I can always lose the weight. Just one step at a time."

"Yeah," said Janice, "he can join a support group to lose weight."

"Hey," I said. "It worked before. Are you still going to AA meetings?"

"Every week."

"And the smoking group?"

"Every week. If I didn't quit smoking, I was going to have to carry around an oxygen bottle."

"I knew a guy who had to use one of them," I said. "He had to remember to shut off the oxygen before lighting up. Otherwise he could blow the place up. The poor guy was in rough shape, but he wouldn't quit smoking. He kept saying it was the only pleasure he had left and that he would die before he would give it up. I guess he did."

"Die?"

"Yeah."

I told my story about giving up smoking. I was a pack-and-a-half corporate soldier in a high-stress, competitive job. That was back when everyone smoked. There were ashtrays everywhere. On every table. Built into the armrests of movie theaters. Next to the urinals to keep guys from throwing in butts. It didn't work, because in every urinal there always floated a few filter tips.

Everyone knew it was bad for their health, but there were only a few crusaders trying to get us to quit. Most of us practiced a form of self-delusion. "Hey, I feel okay and I can quit anytime I want." Until the emphysema got us and the only pleasure we had left was smoking.

I took a Smokenders' class offered by the company as a perk. They let us meet at the office, but we had to pay the full price on the premise that if we paid, we would try harder to get our money's worth. Since I am a cheapskate, that strategy worked for me. The program weaned us off cigarettes slowly by making us aware of the situations in which we smoked. The idea was to short-circuit the habitual smoking patterns one-by-one until there were no occasions to light up.

It was tough. The first assignment was not smoking for 10 minutes after a meal, then 20 minutes, then an hour. Then there was no smoking while drinking coffee. Then while drinking alcohol. Then while driving a car. You get the idea.

The toughest was not smoking while taking a crap. I didn't know if I could take a crap without smoking. Let me tell you, the first time was a strange sensation.

Just after I quit, we moved to Brazil, where everybody smoked. Whenever I met anyone, the first thing they did was offer me a cigarette. There were cigarettes in glass trays in the conference rooms and the coffee server handed out cigarettes with espresso on his hourly circuit around the office.

I made it by eating a lot of great Brazilian food using my rediscovered sense of taste. But within a year, I had gained 20 pounds. On me that is a lot, since my all-time high is only 155 pounds.

We moved back to Ridgefield, Connecticut, after a year. One Sunday morning I was in Squash's, a newsstand where everyone in town went to buy the newspaper. I was cruising the magazine rack when another customer came up to me.

"Hey, Notch," he said. "I haven't seen you for a while. How are Margaret and the kids?"

I had no idea who he was.

He began laughing. "You don't recognize me, do you?"

"Sorry, I don't."

"It's Joe. From Dylan's soccer team."

"Joe?" The Joe that I remembered was a fat, bearded guy that used to joke that he bought his suits at Omar the Tent Maker's. This clean-shaven guy was slightly over average size, but not obese. "What happened?"

"I lost some weight. Seventy pounds."

"Amazing! How did you do it?"

"The Restaurant Diet. All you do is make believe that you are eating every meal in a restaurant. One portion only, and no seconds. I fill my plate in the kitchen and eat in the dining room. No snacking between meals either. It works."

It also worked for me. I lost 30 pounds, getting down to 125 pounds at one point. I have since hovered between 130 and 135 pounds, and it has been more than ten years.

Raz was an improbable guy to have to fight such strong addictions. He seemed pretty straight, but he was a certified alcoholic, a drunk. He was honest enough to admit it, cleaned up his act, and made Chief Petty Officer before retiring from the Coast Guard.

Despite all his difficulties with drinking, he never preached a word of temperance. In fact, he often talked about his drinking days with a kind of nostalgia. And he never said anything when people drank around him. I guess that for Raz, drinking was a personal problem. It was a private struggle that he managed with good humor and a positive attitude. You had to respect that.

Now he was giving up smoking and will have to lose weight. I knew he was going to make it.

17

Tacoma

Raz had a small business making wooden birdhouses that he sold to florists to use in their arrangements. He didn't make much money, but it kept him occupied. He had some deliveries to make and asked if I wanted to go along for the ride. On the way out, we could stop at the Non-Commissioned Officers Club.

The NCO Club had a spartan, military feeling. It was in a long, low building with a pitched roof that reminded me of barracks. Crisply-mowed grass and precisely-trimmed shrubs surrounded the building. The foyer featured a trophy case and a large painting of a destroyer in heavy seas with a wave breaking over her bow. The glossy linoleum floor reflected years of Seaman Apprentice training. The walls were painted a pale institutional green.

I could feel the lonely, echoing quiet that military buildings often have. It was the kind of eternally temporary place that automatically makes me straighten my back and step more briskly.

We went to a steel cafeteria counter and picked up trays that we pushed along, collecting our food from a white-clad mess steward. There were only a few older retirees in the dining room, all dressed in colorful golfing uniforms. Glass doors on one end looked out on the golf course.

The habits I had acquired during my brief Navy days are still strong and I could feel myself relaxing into the familiar order and discipline. The real value of the military lifestyle is the reduction of daily needs to their simplest terms, most of which would be automatically provided for. I never thought of it this way when I was on active duty, but the Navy gave me the space to enjoy the things that matter. Lots of time to ponder the phosphorescence of the bow wake. Or the way the horizon disappears before heavy weather arrives.

It is only when we put aside the rattling complexity and blinding comforts of our lives that we can begin to truly experience each color, smell, sound, taste, and touch. Whether you do it by going to sea, riding a motorcycle across the country, or making a pilgrimage to a holy place, doesn't matter. A quiet mind intensifies life.

I had gone to the University of Puget Sound in Tacoma, a small city just north of Olympia. My recollection of that time was one of continual rainy twilight, a drizzling monotony punctuated by college-level insanity. Margaret wanted to see where I had gone to school, and suggested we make a trip. I was less interested since I had already spent more time there than I cared to.

So we went to Tacoma one afternoon. The school had grown dramatically. There were lots of new buildings and parking lots surrounding the old quad. In the clear yellow sun, the place seemed almost cheerful. Summer session was on and students walked the green paths dressed in bright colors.

It was all wrong.

The only color I remembered during my sojourn was associated with a girl I used to watch from my third-story dorm window. Every day she walked across the misty field to the Student Union wearing a cheerful red raincoat and carrying a matching umbrella. I used to think how beautiful she seemed, although she was an ordinary brunette. Every time I saw her, I fell in love.

The old quad hidden in the center of the expanded campus was unchanged. The red brick buildings with formal gothic arches brought back the boredom and desperation that grew like moss in the endless rainy gloom of Northwest coastal winters. I saw the pine trees still marching on the green and remembered them eternally shrouded in mist and dripping on cringing students as they walked to winter classes.

Somehow, dismal as it was, I preferred my mildewed memory to the postcard scene before me now.

On rare, sunny weekends, I would borrow a friend's motorcycle, a 250cc Honda Dream, and ride the back roads near the school. I used to think, "Wow, it would be great to just keep going."

I had been fantasizing about escaping from school, but this was the first time I had thought of a motorcycle as a way of going to places I had never been, as an instrument of discovery.

Living on an island naturally causes one to think of a motorcycle as a toy. As a way to go fast or as a way to look good. Because on an island, at the end of the day you always end up where you started from. There is just no place to go.

So everyone souped up their bikes with hot cams and high-compression heads and tried to blow away Corvettes, or they chrome-plated them and cruised through drive-ins looking cool.

Now I am riding a slow, weird-looking motorcycle around the country. I have been at it for two months, and still haven't ended up where I started. Cool.

18

Port Orchard

Margaret and I borrowed Raz' car and went to Vancouver to visit one of Margaret's high school friends. On the way to the ferry, we stopped to see another old shipmate, Bill Havens. Bill was a Commissioned Warrant Officer, a main propulsion specialist, one of those exceptionally knowledgeable and indispensable people that keep the Navy underway.

Bill spent most of his career aboard the USS Chipola, home ported at Pearl Harbor and deployed to the Seventh Fleet in the Western Pacific. My first tour in the Navy was aboard the Chipola and I will always be grateful for the experience.

The Chipola was a fleet oiler, a specially-rigged tanker whose primary mission is to refuel ships at sea. This is done while underway, a dangerously exhilarating process, the large ships dancing an intricate tango on the high seas.

First a steel cable is passed to the receiving ship and drawn taut by a winch. Then a six-inch hose is snaked down the cable and the fuel is pumped. All this goes on while the ships steam parallel courses at 15 knots, so close together that if one of the helmsmen sneezed, there might be a collision.

There were so many things that could go wrong, with disastrous consequences. Stepping on a running line could toss a man overboard. Taking a wrong turn on a line could pull a hand into a winch. A line could part, recoiling with enough force to decapitate the crew. Too much tension on a highline could draw a receiving ship too close. Too little would dump the hoses in the water.

The ships might not be able to maintain precisely equal speeds. Or the wind and seas might cause the ships to roll into each other.

Even back then, technology was replacing traditional naval skills such as knots and line handling. But aboard ships like the Chipola, old-fashioned seamanship was everything. Bowlines. Half hitches. Fairleads. Lines faked down on deck so they would run free. More lines aloft than a windjammer. Bosuns piping commands. Bells. McNamara's lace decorating the quarterdeck. "Shipshape" meant something on the Chipola.

Handling the ship while refueling required attention, teamwork and a sea sense learned only on surging decks. It was the kind of stuff that demanded and received the best from all of us.

Our cruise to the Seventh Fleet consisted of taking on cargo fuel in Subic Bay in the Philippines, sailing to Yankee Station in the Tonkin Gulf off the coast of North Vietnam, and refueling aircraft carriers and escort ships while underway. Then it was down the coast of Vietnam into the Gulf of Thailand, refueling as we went, and back up the coast to the carrier to empty our tanks. And on to Subic Bay for one day of liberty.

Since we sailed independently most of the time, we had long periods of quiet routine punctuated by the drama of underway refueling. I had been in the Officer of the Deck watch rotation, one four-hour watch on the bridge with twelve hours off. Most of my time was spent on the cargo deck, the bridge, or my bunk asleep. Bill was on a similar schedule, but all of his time was spent in the engine room, so we seldom saw each other while the ship was underway unless it was in the wardroom for meals or a cup of coffee after standing a late watch.

Sometimes during my watch Bill would call up from the engine room and ask permission to blow stacks. This is a procedure whereby carbon build-up is blown from the smokestack using high-pressure steam. It is probably the origin of the term, "blowing your stack."

Whenever he asked, I had to change course to bring the apparent wind on the beam to avoid getting soot all over the deck. When I got the wind right, I gave the okay to blow. Then I ran to the lee bridge wing to watch the black plume rise out of the stack.

Shortly afterward, Bill would always show up on the bridge. He was built like one of his boilers, a sturdy cylinder of a man, his shirt always drenched with sweat from the heat of the engine room. Bill worked more than twelve hours a day in the roaring engine room. Under hazy artificial light. Breathing the hot oily mist. Checking valves. Listening for unusual sounds in the constant groaning and clanging. He loved it.

"How did it look?" he always asked.

What can one say about soot? "It was black."

"Okay."

Bill and I often went on liberty together. After lunch, we usually went to the officer's club, drank beer, and played the slot machines until happy hour. By the time we finished dinner, we had a full head of steam and were ready for Olongapo.

Since officers could go ashore in civilian clothes, we were easily spotted and usually ignored by the pimps and hustlers who hovered just beyond the no-man's-land outside the main gate. Bell-bottom sailors were easier marks than officers and chiefs.

But the moneychangers surrounded us. Outstretched fists holding bundles of pesos. All of them pleading the same rate in anxious voices. I picked one of the hungrier looking ones and handed him a ten. The others immediately stepped away. We breathed again.

Sometimes we took cartons of Marlboro cigarettes that we bought for $1 in the Ship's Store while at sea. Marlboros could get almost anything you wanted. A couple of cartons could last all night.

The main street felt like the Wild West. It had a loose, no-holds-barred ambiance. A rough-edged, beer-soaked irreverence. I had always expected to see a sheriff, his hat pulled down over his eyes, his hand on his gun, leaning against a doorway silently watching. Or maybe a body flying through the swinging doors of the saloon.

Some of the buildings had second story balconies that cantilevered over the sidewalk. Others had stepped facades hiding simple pitched roofs made of rusting corrugated iron. There were hostess bars with olive-skinned girls from up-country pushing drinks for a small commission. Regular bars with few amenities but lots of cheap beer. Pawnshops, massage parlors, barbershops, curio stores, tattoo parlors. And street vendors selling everything from snacks smelling of coconut oil to cheap trinkets.

The whorehouses and cockfight arenas were hidden in the maze of low houses that spread out from the main street like a bloodstain. There was even a jai alai fronton we once walked to, through damp smelling streets too small for a car to pass.

We always went to the same bar, on the second floor of a long, rambling building on the main drag. The bar consisted of a cooler the length of the building. It was filled with green San Miguel beer and ice. Vendors wandered among the tables selling monkey meat barbecued on a stick. And balut, chicken embryo still in the egg. They put the eggs in front of a candle to show the embryos. Drunken sailors bought them to eat on dares. They always threw up shortly afterward. Occasionally, a hopeless young girl would come by selling flowers.

We sat courageously around a table in the warm alcoholic mist and told lies like fishermen. Once, to prove the watches we had just bought while on R&R in Hong Kong were really waterproof, we dumped them into a pitcher of beer. My Rolex Oyster Perpetual had cost $25. The next morning I checked my watch as the ship was getting underway. The crystal was completely fogged over. It quit running a few days later. And, yes, we drank the beer in the pitcher before we fished the watches out.

When Bill retired 15 years ago, he and his wife Betty drove a homemade pickup camper across the country. They stopped to see us on the way.

They were on a '60s-style grand tour, inexpensive and exuberant. When they were not visiting friends, they slept in the camper. They laughed and talked their way across the country, honoring old experiences while creating new ones to remember. I was just starting a corporate career. Wearing a three-piece suit. Beginning to realize what I had gotten into. I was envious.

Bill looked like an old salt, a solidly-built man with the patina of years at sea. He didn't have the awkwardness that men accustomed to wearing uniforms often have when they first retire. In fact, he looked like he had always worn denim and flannel.

Betty had long hair that she allowed to take on the iron tones of middle age. She used no make-up and wore sensible earthy clothes that flowed like a ballad by Joan Baez. She was a cheerfully unrepentant hippie. An artist.

They matched.

I have noticed that career military people don't seem to get too cynical or jaded. Maybe the spartan quality of military life lets them maintain the innocence of their youth. Military life seldom allows people to indulge pointless desires. They don't give up half their lives covering their ass at the office so they can build their dream house only to sit alone in the elegant formal living room and say, "So what?" Or buy an expensive Hasselblad only to find that they still don't take very many pictures. Or take a luxury Mediterranean cruise only to get drunk and pig out every night because of boredom. Or buy a brand-new BMW only to constantly worry about parking it where it won't get dinged. Or, worse, to spend all the time washing and polishing it.

So Bill and Betty came to see us fresh and hopeful, with a new life ahead of them. But they had only about ten years before Betty got cancer and died. The retirement they had anticipated for so long ended like being jerked awake in the middle of a pleasant dream. Bill wrote us a long, painful letter telling us what had happened. At the time, he had been mourning. Now, only three years later, I didn't know what to expect.

We turned into his driveway, went past the old house on the street, and up to the new house in back. Two children ran across the yard, shouting, "They're here!"

The place was out of the '60s. Flower Power. Laid back. Taking it as it comes. I could tell that Betty had a lot to do with building it.

The house by the street needed paint but appeared happily occupied. The yard behind was inspired more by *The Mother Earth News* than *House and Garden*. There were lots of flowers and a vegetable garden behind the bumpy lawn. Bill's home had a natural finish that blended easily into the evergreen hill behind the house.

Bill came out the door. He still had his stocky frame and the same mischievous eyes. His grin was hidden behind a Van Dyke beard that, with his balding head, gave him the expression of a jolly sorcerer. He was smoking a small cigar with a white plastic tip.

Bill's two daughters, one of whom lived in Bill's old house by the street, joined us with the children. We went through a round of introductions, Bill proudly naming each of his grandchildren.

"We were picking strawberries," said one of the little ones.

That launched us on a tour of the garden. We looked at the raspberries, strawberries, and lush vegetables crowding each other, hobby roses and secret places for kids to hide.

We went back into the house and Bill showed us the rock collection he was beginning. Amateur geology didn't seem quite right for someone who spent all of his life on the water. Then I watched Bill and the children pick through the stones and point out marks and bits of color. Of course! Bill was a grandfather. "I'm going to get me one of those rock tumblers," said Bill. "Then I can polish these stones up. We go out on rock hunting trips. It's a great way to see the country and the kids have fun."

"Hey," said Bill, "I have something to show you." He picked up a stack of photographs from the table. They were black-and-white enlargements of the Chipola taken from aircraft and other ships. Most of them showed the ship during underway replenishment. One dramatic shot showed the Chipola alongside an aircraft carrier to port and a destroyer to starboard, with all the hoses and highlines deployed.

The surging excitement of those times came rushing back to me.

"What happened to the Chipola?" I asked.

"Decommissioned right here in Bremerton. I was with the crew that brought her in. Afterward, I asked to be assigned to the mothball fleet for my last tour before retirement."

So Bill had lost the two most important things in his life.

"Granddad's talking about the Navy again," said one of the children.

"Can I wear your hat?" said another child.

"No, let me."

Bill held his Naval officer's hat above their heads. "You take turns."

"You want to come up to the bridge?" asked Bill. "I had it built into the house."

We followed him up a circular stairway to an open room with a glass wall that looked out onto Puget Sound. There was a compass binnacle centered on a wall that looked like a conning station. But there was no ship's wheel or engine room telegraph. A pair of binoculars sat on a small table. It was the bridge of a ship cruising in the past, with no helm to guide it. A ship with both engines backing and no way to signal, "All ahead full."

"I come up here a lot," said Bill. "I like to watch the traffic on the Sound."

But I knew he did it because he missed the sea. He had not, since Betty's death, found anything to replace the intensity of his life aboard the Chipola.

We spent the afternoon talking story and playing with the children. Betty was so much a part of the place and our conversation, I felt we were visiting her also.

Bill's Christmas card a year later read, "Got me a new computer, got me a new woman, gonna move to Texas and raise emus." It took him a while, but he got back underway. Like I said, he was a main propulsion specialist.

19

Headed North

It was decision time. Up till now, when people asked me where I was going, I always said, "The West Coast, and maybe Alaska." I always said, "maybe," so if I gave up when I got to the West Coast I could still say, "I did it."

Funny, nobody ever heard the "maybe." They always responded, "Wow, Alaska! I wish I could go there." As though they knew I didn't have a choice. That giving up was impossible.

I was going to Alaska.

Before heading north, the bike needed some attention. The rear tire was worn to the replacement indicators. The front tire was still okay, but would probably need replacement while in Alaska. And the oil and filter needed changing.

I found a BMW dealer in Tacoma, just off the interstate. I called and explained that I was passing through and needed service. They said to come over anytime, that no appointment was necessary for people on the road.

I rode up the next morning and they got the bike into the shop right away. I looked through the showroom while I was waiting. None of the bikes interested me, but I saw a guy dressed in an expensive leather BMW riding suit and matching BMW riding boots. He carried a BMW System helmet that cost at least three times what my Shoei did.

Every now and then, all the BMW brand marketing pays off, and here was an example of their success. I felt sure this guy also had a BMW coffee cup, beer mug, Cross pen, pencil holder, mouse pad, T-shirt, golf sweater, sweatshirt, ball cap, belt buckle, and watch.

We met at a yellow and black bumblebee version of my motorcycle. "How do you like your GS?" he asked. He must have seen me come in.

"Great."

"I ride a K1," he said proudly. "It's outside." It was an invitation to look at his machine.

The K1 is the most expensive BMW motorcycle, a Teutonic crotch rocket with four cylinders, fuel injection, water-cooling, full bodywork, and clip-on handlebars. It was a nice try, but Hondas at half the price outrun the K1, and they handle better too. On the other hand, my GS is the cheapest BMW motorcycle, entry level, and strictly low-tech. I was happy to concede that he stood at the top of the BMW hill so I just said, "Nice."

He was disappointed in my lack of interest, but he perked up and said with the authority suitable to his status, "This is a great dealership. First-class work."

"Are you here for service?" I thought I might have preempted his appointment.

"No, I just came here to check out the bikes." He looked at me suspiciously and asked, "Are you going to Alaska?"

"Yes."

"Where are you from?"

"New York."

"So how long have you been on the road?"

"Two months."

"Did you have any trouble with the bike?"

"None that wasn't my fault."

"The Boxers are great machines." he said, patting the seat of the GS. "Tell me about your trip. I wish I could do something like that."

Scratch a yuppie and you usually find a real person underneath.

I bought my tent from L.L. Bean before leaving on the trip. The aluminum tent poles had bent into a permanent curve after a short time and Bean replaced them while I was in Houston. A month later, in Olympia, they were bent again.

So I called Bean and asked for another set of tent poles. Instead, they sent me a more expensive tent at no extra charge, saying that the tent they originally sold me was not intended for my kind of use. I should have gotten an expedition model. They said it was their fault for misadvising me and apologized for the inconvenience. Amazing.

I had to stay an extra day after Margaret left to wait for the new tent, but I was happy for an excuse to avoid leaving. Getting back on the road after a layover is like forcing yourself to go to the gym for a workout. You know you need it and will feel better afterward, but it would be really nice to skip it just this one time.

I worried that I was becoming complacent. The initial novelty of the ride had faded. Life on the road was becoming routine. I was no longer afraid of the bike or uncertain of my skills.

It was getting dangerous.

I had been using my fear like salt, to enhance the flavor of the ride, to keep me focused and safe. Now I needed some other way to get back into The Ride. Alaska had to be it.

The new tent arrived as promised. The next morning I got on the motorcycle, waved good-bye to Raz, Janice, and Auntie as they stood in the driveway, and rode reluctantly to the expressway headed north to Seattle and the Canadian border.

My plan was to follow I-5 to Route 512, bypassing Tacoma, and picking up Route 167, which joined I-405, bypassing Seattle. I-405 led to Route 9, a two-lane road headed north to the Canadian border. Everything up to Route 9 was expressway, but I would avoid the major commuter routes. There were no two-lane alternatives.

This was more planning than I had done on the entire trip. Unfortunately, it didn't work.

I missed the Route 512 exit because I was in the high-speed commuter lane to avoid the trucks that took up the two right-hand lanes. That took me through Tacoma at rush hour. I stopped at a rest stop to check the map and saw I could get on Route 167 at the next exit. But the next exit was marked Route 164, so I kept going. No Route 167.

As I was approaching Seattle, I saw I-405 and followed it, remembering that it bypassed Seattle. I needed a rest stop to check the map. Badly. I exited into downtown Renton. One-way streets. No parking. Traffic lights on every corner. I spent at least a half-hour trying to find the entrance ramp to get back on the expressway.

I rushed north on I-5. My side of the highway was clear, but the southbound lanes were still crowded with the morning migration into the city. I needed to get back on a simple two-lane road. There was too much anger flowing uninterrupted on the wide, smooth highway. Too many people rushing to places they really didn't want to go to, half-listening to some airhead jabber the bad news on the radio. Worrying about being late again. Looking straight ahead to avoid eye contact. The morning smell of warming asphalt and exhaust fumes. Drinking coffee from a spill-proof mug. A sour feeling in the stomach already.

I was reminded that I was still on the West Coast as I set up camp next to what probably was a Gold Wing. It was big enough to be a Gold Wing, but it had a fitted cover so I wasn't sure. A camping trailer was set up next to the bike. Outside the door of the trailer, two lawn chairs were carefully arranged on an Astroturf carpet.

A couple came out of the trailer with a tiny portable TV. They fiddled with the antenna until the picture was clear. Then they settled into their lawn chairs and watched the flickering blue screen as I set up my tent on the hard packed dirt. We never spoke, not even to exchange greetings. I could feel the invisible wall they seemed to have erected between our campsites.

After dinner I sat at my grease-stained picnic table and worked on my journal. Up the way there was another Gold Wing with a camping trailer. It had the obligatory lawn chairs in front of the door. Plus, the bike had a sidecar. The motorcycle, sidecar, and trailer had been painted and pinstriped in exactly the same color and style.

The sidecar rig should have won easily. But, after considering the Astroturf and TV next to me, I declared it a standoff.

20

Canada

In the morning it was cool and still. Water beaded on the tent fly as though it had rained. A heavy dew. My shoes were drenched from walking through the grass to the restroom.

I expected green early morning freshness, but there was only the heavy, sour smell of sewage in the air. There must have been a problem with the pump-out station for the rows of RVs parked in the grassy meadow next to the office.

I was out of there before the Gold Wing riders were stirring.

I ended up crossing into Canada on Route 539 instead of Route 9, as I had expected. The customs station looked like a toll-booth. It was just wide enough for a car to pass through. A sign said, "Please wait behind the line until the car ahead is finished."

Beyond the customs station, in Canada, was a low administrative building.

I rode up to the booth and presented my passport.

"Where are you going in Canada?"

"The Alaska Highway."

"Are you going to Alaska?"

"Yes."

"Do you have any weapons with you?"

"No."

The customs officer handed back my passport and pointed to the administrative building. "Please drive over there and wait for an officer."

Shit. Now what? I put my passport away and rode the bike to the building.

Another customs officer came out of the building and instructed me to park the bike and remove the saddlebags. He inspected both saddlebags and the tent bag on the luggage rack. I had to remove the seat to get out my registration and insurance card so he even looked into the toolbox under the seat.

When he was done he said, "Okay," and went back into the building, leaving me with everything strewn on the ground.

Since I had come across the border on a different road than I had intended, I had no idea how to get to Route 7. I also noticed at the border that I had lost the valve cap on my front tire.

After wandering around in the general vicinity of Route 7 for a while, I stopped at a Honda motorcycle dealership and asked for a valve cap and directions.

They gave me both, free, and I was soon winding along the Frazer River, through little Canadian villages. I was surprised by the strong sense of being in a foreign country. Speed limits and distances in kilometers. A unique vocal inflection with a question at the end of each sentence, eh? A subtly different color palette. Strong colors, but muted rather than watered into pastels. Boxy, practical houses suggesting severe winters. Signs in French and English. Business names ending in Ltd. Vaguely colonial, still, after all the years of independence.

Beyond Harrison Hot Springs, I got the ride back. The deserted road wound along the Frazer River through a soft pine forest that muted the engine into a murmur that flowed with the river. I leaned left and right, downshifting going in and accelerating out of the turns. Swinging to the rhythm of the road. I could feel the tightness in my shoulders loosen as the bike rode itself through the curves.

I stopped for lunch at a roadside restaurant just outside of Agassi. It was in a small bungalow, stained dark brown, behind a parking lot that had only two cars in it. The dining room had less than ten tables arranged close together. An old, very fat man sat at one of the tables holding a cane with one hand, as though he needed to support himself even while sitting. He was wearing a dirty gray T-shirt that swelled over his belly.

"You should get a Jeep," he was saying to a pretty woman in a conservative dress sitting at the next table. "Or a convertible. That'll get the guys' attention."

"You still have a good figure," he continued. "You should show it off."

She blushed and started laughing as though she had just thought of a dirty joke while talking to a preacher. She struggled to control herself, her hand over her mouth.

"You won't get much attention sitting inside a Nissan sedan."

She finally laughed out loud. She looked over at me and shook her head. "He's a real character," she said.

She stood up and I saw the old goat was right. She did have a good figure.

"I have to go," she said, still laughing.

After she left, the old man turned to me and said, "I talk to all the women that come into this place. She was a good one."

I ordered the lunch special, Manhattan clam chowder, potato salad, and a grilled cheese sandwich on dark bread. The owner of the restaurant took my order back to his wife in the kitchen. He returned with my soup and sat at the table with me.

"Are you going to Alaska?" he asked. His accent was vaguely German, but not as harsh and clipped. Probably Scandinavian. A lot of them migrated here because the climate and the landscape is similar to their homeland.

"I'm on my way."

"Do you have mosquito repellent?" asked the old man. "You are going to need it up there. Some of the bugs are as big as birds."

"Be sure to stop in Agassi and buy some," said the owner. "It gets more expensive as you get further north. Everything gets more expensive, but bug spray is like gold up there."

The owner's wife brought out my lunch. "A lot of people who stopped here this year were going to Alaska," she said.

"It's the 50th Anniversary of the Alaska Highway," said the old man. "A lot of the men who worked on it are coming back for a reunion."

Oh, no. I had to pick the year of the big reunion.

"Most of those guys must be over 70, if the road is 50 years old," I said. I was starting to feel better.

"I guess they are getting old, like me. I don't get around much anymore. So I just sit here and let the world come to me."

"We meet a lot of interesting people here. So many stories."

"Yes it's lots of fun. We keep this place small so that we can talk to everybody. That's more important than making a lot of money."

I wanted to stay and talk story but I had to get pretty far north that afternoon. It was 200 miles to the next campground. I left reluctantly, surprised that I had spent almost two hours in the place.

All morning I had been headed east along the Frazer River, running against its final rush through the green coastal mountains to end in the Straits of Juan de Fuca. I followed as the river turned abruptly north.

Suddenly, the landscape opened as though it was spreading its arms in a welcoming gesture. I was in a wide desert valley surrounded by brown hillsides dotted with dark green shrubs.

The river ran blue and green down the center of the valley, powerful and fast, none of its strength tapped by thirsty plants. The banks of the river consisted of dirt and stone. Small tufts of grass were bleached almost white by the sun. The sky was entirely blue except for a small white smear, like a thumbprint, near the horizon.

For me, deserts are places of energy and renewal, places where there are pillars of fire and where saviors seek the divine. I was glad to be in this arid, empty place.

The sudden warmth after a relaxing lunch made me sleepy so I pulled into a rest stop. I found a picnic table and lay down on the warm boards and dozed, dreaming desert thoughts.

I heard the loping, irregular beat of a Harley approaching. The sound cut as the bike turned, then stuttered through a downshift. I kept my eyes closed, listening to the thumping idle and the final gasp as the engine died.

Harley music is unmistakable. A glorious four-stroke symphony. A purely mechanical sound of the carb sucking air, valves clicking, gasoline exploding, and chains rattling—all in an uneven V-twin cadence. Listen carefully and you can hear every step in the process of converting gasoline into forward motion.

I felt a shadow over my face and opened my eyes. A young couple was looking down at me.

The girl was a pretty blonde, slightly built, wearing a black leather motorcycle jacket. The guy had black, spiky hair pressed down in places by his helmet. He was wearing a plain white T-shirt. He seemed vaguely Oriental, probably American Indian.

"Hi," said the blonde. "That looks comfortable."

I sat up. "I needed the rest."

"I was getting sleepy, too," said the Indian. "It got so warm."

"Are you on your way to Alaska?"

How does everyone know? "Yes."

"Are you taking the ferry?"

"On the way back. I want to ride up on the Alaska Highway."

"Too bad. We're headed to Prince Rupert. We could have ridden with you part of the way."

I glanced at their bike. It had only a small duffel bag attached to the sissy bar. "Are you going to Alaska?"

"No. We live in Terrace, just outside of Prince Rupert. We took the ferry to Vancouver and spent a few days. We're headed home now."

Maybe they could give me some pointers. "Have you been to Alaska?"

"No, but we really want to go. There's never enough time," said the blonde.

"Funny, there is always plenty of time to work and hang around at home watching TV, but never enough time to do what you really want," said the Indian. "How do you manage it?"

"I just took off. I guess I sort of dropped out. I was sick of the BS and I had a chance to make a break, so I took it."

"Alright!"

We talked and rested for a while then got back on our bikes and rode on. Later, I realized I never got their names. They seemed so much like old friends that introductions seemed unnecessary.

There were only a few cars on the road and most of the time I was riding alone. The air was so clear that I seemed to be looking through binoculars. In the distance, I saw a couple of helicopters flying back and forth between the hillside and the river. It was a long time before I could determine what was going on. A pickup truck and a sedan were parked along the road, their occupants standing outside, pointing at a brush fire on the hillside. I parked behind them. The helicopters hovered over the river like honey-bees, drawing water through long hoses. When their tanks were full, they lumbered to the hillside and sprayed the fire.

I felt as though I was watching the operation on TV with the sound turned off. We were very far from the action. The helicopters looked like toys and the fire was a dark blur, almost invisible in the distance. There was hardly any smoke except for tiny white billows when the helicopters sprayed their water.

We were excited. This was the only activity in the entire desolate landscape, and we made the most of it. We commented knowledgeably about brush fires as though we had spent our lives observing them. We wondered about the water capacity of the helicopters and how long it took to fill their tanks. And we discussed the efficiency of the helicopter method of fighting brush fires compared to, say, lighting backfires.

But it was a small fire so we ran quickly through our routines. The four-wheelers stretched and hitched up their pants. "Well, gotta go. See ya." We dispersed, grateful for the diversion.

When I arrived at my assigned campsite at Cache Creek campground, I found a couple setting up a tent. I tried to explain that I had been assigned the site and showed them my receipt. Their car had Oregon plates but they did not understand English. We struggled for a while, gesturing and shrugging our shoulders, nodding and shaking our heads. They broke out occasionally for consultations in rapid-fire French. I understood a little, but was too embarrassed to try speaking. I always forget most of my limited vocabulary as soon as I have to speak.

My language problem comes from having grown up in a bilingual family whose members each spoke only one language. My grandmother understood English well, but she only spoke Japanese. The rest of us understood some Japanese, but we only spoke English. Every morning began something like:

"Ohio gozaimas."

"Hi Obaban."

"Ikaga deska?"

"Oh, pretty good."

To this day, I automatically respond in English whenever I am spoken to in Japanese or any other language.

French-Canadians? Europeans? Oregon plates? The man fair-skinned and blue-eyed. The woman a mulatto, olive-skinned with large, sultry features. I bet there was an interesting story there.

We went back to the office and I explained the problem. I was assigned the next space and left the foreign couple to pantomime with the campground owner. I suspected they thought they could camp without paying.

I woke when the sun lit the side of the tent. That turned out to be pretty early this far north, so I was on the road by 8:00. The road was deserted and I was able to make good time, traveling about 80 mph across the open desert. I let the bike find its own pace as I watched the morning rotate the shadows and brighten the eastern hillsides.

Beyond Quesnel the road began climbing the foothills of the Rockies. The warm desert colors began fading into dark green pine forest, like the last bit of sunset stretched out over a hundred miles.

I saw a roadside vendor in a small parking area and decided to stop. He was in a delivery truck with a window cut into the side. A steel awning shaded the window. The menu was scrawled on a dusty chalkboard with the ghosts of earlier offerings underneath. I bought a root beer float, a scoop of vanilla ice cream in a paper cup and a bottle of root beer.

I walked back to the road and sat on a fence. The road was straight for about a quarter-mile, then it curved gently to the left. A policeman had set up a speed trap and was clocking people as they came around the curve, stopping them almost in front of me. I watched the drivers waiting in their cars as the policeman approached, their heads bowed and their arms extended, hands clutching the top of the steering wheel. One tried to argue with the policeman, turning and gesturing as the officer bent over the window. The others mutely passed over their papers and took their tickets, keeping their eyes down and nodding when questioned.

Two men joined me for the afternoon entertainment. They were dressed in thick flannel shirts and blue jeans faded almost white over their knees. Both had ice cream cones.

"That policeman's pretty busy this afternoon, eh?"

"Got three since I've been sitting here," I replied. "I feel a little embarrassed watching."

"I know what you mean. We could be the ones getting a ticket."

"Did you ride that motorbike all the way from New York?"

"Yes."

"I was in New York in 1969. That was enough for me. I don't know how people can live so crowded together."

Many people think New York City and New York State are the same. "I don't live in the city. I live in upstate New York. It's pretty rural there."

"Yeah. I never saw so many people in one place, not even at the World's Fair in Seattle. I was there too."

I decided not to disturb his myth. After all, he had been there.

I imagined him being bumped by the crowd while trying to read the news ticker in Times Square. In 1969 he wouldn't have been so old. Maybe he went there with the same wonder and excitement I felt the first time I went to the city. Maybe it was just his memory that had gotten old.

21

The Alaska Highway

The next morning's ride passed through blue alpine country-side in the upper end of the Rocky Mountain range. Black snow-striped mountains. Velvet dark-green pine forests. A dream trout stream rushing fast and white, then resting in dark pools and rippling eddies. Approaching Dawson Creek, I noticed fields with rolls of hay whitening against the vibrating green grass. It was an exhilarating ride, like reaching and stretching, working out the kinks in the body.

Dawson Creek is the southern end of the Alaska Highway. Milepost 0. There is a nondescript monument in the middle of a featureless square marking the exact spot. All the buildings surrounding the square were low and the place felt incomplete, as though the builders said, "This will do, we can build a proper place later, when we have time."

The frontier is never quite finished, always abandoned for the next unexplored place. In this sense, this square was an appropriate beginning for the road of dreams. The Alcan. The ultimate adventure road. Great trips start in dull places. Isn't that why we go?

I wanted an early stop so I rode only to Fort St. John on a perfectly ordinary two-lane highway. Not much of a challenge so far.

I walked to the center of town where there was an oil derrick in the middle of a barren, treeless park. There was a bandstand next to the derrick with a banner that read "Doings at the Derrick."

A group of gospel music singers wearing dark red robes was performing to a large crowd. They sang with their eyes closed and their heads bent back at a slight angle, blowing a spiritual wind that swayed the crowd.

A preacher wearing a golf shirt with horizontal blue stripes and gray slacks slipping below his potbelly, introduced the hymns and encouraged the audience to participate. His performance was mechanical, as though he was lip-synching to a tape recording made too long ago.

When the people sang they held their hands in the air and shuffled to the ancient rhythms. There were lots of young people in the crowd. A second preacher wearing dark aviator-style glasses walked onto the stage with his arms raised. He was born again, brothers and sisters, and Jesus had changed his life.

The morning's ride was pine cold, the chill enlarged by the shade green and silent dampness. At the first rest stop I put on my sweater and heavy gloves. At the next I switched to leather.

Pine forest crowded the shoulders of the road except where it was ripped by clear cutting. The trees were cut back to precise borders, intensifying the brutality of the clear-cutting procedure. Loggers argue that clear-cutting is like a forest fire, nature's way of rejuvenating the land. But even when it is most destructive, nature marks the land with irregular, random strokes. The scene of a forest fire can be beautiful in its wildness.

A clear-cut area is simply ugly. Too orderly, square-cornered, and straight-edged. Too evenly mowed, like a suburban lawn. One thinks of two-car garages, center-entrance colonials and legal-size paper for insurance policies.

Fire is better.

The road was good except for a short section of gravel that was under repair. An approaching bus didn't slow down and threw dust and stones all over me.

I smelled gas at one point and came upon an oilfield, the black pumps nodding in a tangle of silver pipes and tanks.

By 11:00 I was 100 miles up the road and halfway to Fort Nelson. I stopped for lunch at a one of the truck stops that appeared at 50-mile intervals. There were no other signs of habitation on the road. The truck stops provide everything one needs to sustain life on the road. Gasoline, tire repair, showers, video games, coffee refills for the thermos, and road food served cafeteria-style to eat inside or as you drive. I had vegetable beef soup served in a Styrofoam cup, an egg salad sandwich wrapped in clear plastic, and coffee for $2.89.

The ride into Fort Nelson was straight and fast. Although it was level, I had the feeling of traveling through the tree line on a mountain. The trees began to thin out and grew shorter. Brown edged and silvery moss carpeted the forest floor. The wildflowers were hot violet, not quite pink. The exact shade of the motorcycle. Nearby hills fell away into black mountain ranges behind.

I stopped at the Information Center in Fort Nelson, but was put off by the recitation of local attractions made up for the tourists. I decided instead to continue on to Steamboat, 50 miles up the road.

The road to Steamboat goes through the lowest point on the Alaska Highway, before starting a hilly, winding climb back into the Rocky Mountains. Parts of the original highway were being replaced by a straight modern road that left brown scars on the hillsides and mounds of fill in the valleys. The old road crossed the new occasionally, softly winding around obstacles and over hills. I wanted to try the old road but it was already abandoned and the intersections had been blocked.

Steamboat turned out to be a gas station and snack bar in a small clearing. I was told I could camp on the grass next to the snack bar for $5. Pit toilets, no showers. Nobody else, either, which was fine with me. There was a comforting view of the mist-blue and green valley below.

I set up the tent and went to dinner. I had exactly the same thing as lunch, vegetable beef soup and an egg salad sandwich. Except the soup was in a big crockery bowl and hearty enough to be a main course, and the sandwich came on thick slabs of home-made bread.

Everything was homemade because of the remoteness of the area. Supplies were delivered once a week from Fort Nelson, except in winter, when the road was often closed.

The wind shifted during the night and I was choked awake by the stench of the outhouse. It was a big, potent smell, slimy black and impossible to sleep through.

I buried my head in the sleeping bag and tried to filter the air. It didn't help. I tried to breathe shallowly thinking less air would mean less smell. It doesn't. I started to get a headache.

I had to get out of there.

Although it was only 4:00 a.m., it was fairly light, with the sun slanting up from below the horizon. I packed, trying to hold my breath and breathing in shallow bursts. The smell left a salty, dirty taste in my mouth. It took a while for the mountain air to blow the smell out of my nostrils. My mouth and lungs seemed coated with a potent slime. Everything was polluted. My hair, clothes, sleeping bag, and tent.

Sitting in a far corner drinking coffee at the first truck stop, I felt like someone who had just come out of the subway on a humid summer day, a mildewed old smell wafting off of me like demented perfume. After I had washed up and brushed my teeth, I felt better.

I rounded a wide curve and found a group of RVs and cars parked along the road. People had gotten out and were taking pictures and pointing at the hillside. A herd of mountain sheep was picturesquely posed among the rocks. It was as though the Alaska Highway Tourist Board had arranged this photo opportunity. A Kodak moment.

I slowed and waved at the sheep, but didn't stop.

The countryside became more and more like the pictures in the tourist brochures. Rocky mountains rising behind incredibly blue lakes. Trout streams winding through broad gravel valleys. Streams sometimes as blue as the sky, other times so clear the rocky bottoms seemed to reflect on the surface like a mirror image.

Magnificent. Unbelievable. And, after a while, overwhelming. Too much natural beauty and the mind begins to shut down. I started stopping at valley overlooks trying to find caribou. Never mind the crystal air and the mountain light that seemed to come from everywhere at once. Forget the blue-gray rocky peaks in the background, fringed with snow. How come there were no caribou? The brochures showed herds of them in valleys just like these.

A kid wearing a black Harley-Davidson T-shirt and a leather wallet on a silver chain came up to me at the gas pump. "Wow! What kind of bike is this?"

"A BMW."

"Gigantic tank! How much gas does it hold?"

"Five and a half gallons."

"Whoa! No chain."

"Paralever."

"What's that?"

"Shaft drive with universal joints on both ends and a torque bar. Keeps the rear end from rising. It rides like a chain-drive bike with all the advantages of a shaft drive."

"Wow! That blows my mind!"

He went through the entire motorcycle like this, in incredible detail. He wanted to understand everything he saw.

I knew he was dreaming, waiting for the day he could get his own bike. I remembered when I wanted every bike I saw, when I agonized over every detail as I chose my dream bike.

I devoured every magazine, reading each one more closely than a lawyer reads a contract. I stopped and looked at every bike I came across. Triumph, BSA, Norton, Harley-Davidson? Big single, vertical twin, V-twin? Café, Euro, or American-style handlebars? Split gas tanks? Saddlebags? High pipes? Dual or single carbs? I put more intensity into choosing my dream than into any bike I had actually bought.

I had to support the kid. Plus, I enjoyed being the cool, expert rider.

I took the waters at Liard Hot Springs, walking the half-mile from the empty parking lot to the springs. There was a small changing hut where I left my clothes. I was worried about leaving my wallet, but other people had left their clothes in neat piles on the benches.

The spring fed into three pools, each a bit cooler going downstream. I started in the lower pool. It was like a hot bath. The water was perfectly clear and the bottom was clean gray stone. The vegetation was almost tropical.

A couple with two small children were in the pool. The kids were complaining that the water smelled funny. It had a slightly sulphurous smell.

I moved to the next pool, which was considerably warmer. Two college girls on a summer trip to Alaska were trying to decide where to stop for the night. Here at the Lodge or on to Watson Lake? They were surprised that I was riding a motorcycle and camping.

The spring emptied directly into the top pool. A gray-haired man boiled bright red was getting out as I slipped in. "Don't stay in too long," he said. "It's hot."

It was, and I could stay in only a few minutes before retreating to the second pool. I soaked until the smell of last night was finally gone, then got out loose-limbed and weak, ready for a nap.

The road levels out past Liard and I was starting to make some time when I saw the flashing lights behind me. Shit! I stopped on the dirt shoulder and lifted my face shield.

A uniformed Mountie appeared next to me. "Can I see your driver's license and registration?"

I settled the bike on the sidestand and took my wallet from my jacket pocket. What the hell, I thought, I wasn't going that fast. I handed him my license.

"I have to take off the seat to get my registration." I started to get off the bike.

"That's okay. I'm just going to give you a warning ticket. You were doing 60 in a 50 zone."

Ah, it was motorcycle harassment time. Any excuse to stop a biker and check him out. I guess I passed inspection.

"You don't have to do anything about this ticket. You don't have to notify your insurance company or anything. Just throw it away."

Why bother writing it then? "Okay."

"Have a nice day."

22

Yukon Territory

Watson Lake, just over the line in Yukon Territory, was the main staging area during the construction of the Alaska Highway.

Today it is a tourist trap. Expensive hotels with rooms beginning at $65. A Signpost Forest in a fenced area with a tall gate, containing elaborately-painted signs indicating the distances to places like Paducah and Sacramento. A nightly Canteen Show recreating the wartime USO shows with music and skits from the 1940s. Tired girls dying for a cigarette in the Information Centre. The parking lot full of RVs.

I wandered around the Signpost Forest looking for a sign for Rochester or Honolulu. It was very poorly organized. They should group things in alphabetical order or by state and country. Or at least provide an index and a map.

I gave up quickly, having once again failed at being a tourist, and rode on, looking for a campground.

Halfway up the Alaska Highway and the road has become everything. Adventurers, travelers, tourists, and everyone serving them—all here because of the road. Gas station villages including a café, lodge, hot showers, gift shop, groceries, and RV wash. Towns whose entire industry is the road. More hotel rooms and restaurant seats than permanent residents. Tour guides relentlessly telling the same story to the endless stream of people passing through.

I travel alone most of the time because the motor homes and truck-bed campers tend to bunch up in little herds. The trick is to stay between them, stopping for a break when I catch up and moving fast enough to stay ahead of the herd behind.

I took one of my breaks at an idyllic rest stop next to a stream. I parked behind a large motor home and walked to a picnic table by the water.

A woman came by with a bucket, which she silently filled at the stream. Hmm. A few minutes later, she came back for more water.

I followed her after the third bucket. She took the water to a man on a short ladder scrubbing the front of the motor home with a long-handled brush. They were washing the damn thing!

I looked at the front of my bike. It was a sticky-looking smear of dead bugs, asphalt, and gray mud. The wheels were caked in mud and there was junk caught in the cooling fins on the engine. Mud flaked off the exhaust pipes like peeling paint. It looked fine to me.

Winter raises hell with the road. Frost heaves leave sections of it looking like an artillery range, and a lot of it has to be regraded each year. Pavement heaves just as bad as dirt and is harder to fix, so most of the road consisted of sealcoat, liquid asphalt sprayed right over graded dirt. The sealcoat kept the dust down and provided a fairly hard surface after it had been rolled in by the traffic.

There was a lot of grading going on. Traffic was stopped on both ends of the section of road being worked on. Groups of vehicles were led through behind a pickup truck with a flashing light and a large sign that read, "Follow Me."

Most of the time the sections being graded were just dusty. Sometimes a water truck sprayed the road to hold down the dust and it was muddy. Sometimes we drove over fresh asphalt and the tires felt sticky. Sometimes it was very soft and I had trouble keeping up enough speed to avoid bogging down. The knobby tires helped.

Away from Watson Lake, it felt more like the Yukon Territory
I imagined. The Wild West. An Indian came over to me at dinner
and said, "Hello Wong." His voice had the yeasty scent of too
much beer.

He put his hand on my shoulder to steady himself. His
shadow rocked across the table. "Doing a lot of writing, eh,
Wong?"

I was working on my journal.

He stepped back into the aisle and swayed into the restroom.
The man at the next table said, "Damn Indians! They can't hold
their liquor."

The night clouds were blue-black and gray lying on the horizon. The sun somewhere behind made vibrating shafts of light
above and below the clouds. Triangular patterns all over the sky.

In the morning, during breakfast, two men came into the restaurant speaking French. The waitress said angrily, "Speak English! This is Canada! Speak English!"

There was a hand lettered sign above the cashier's head,
"Cigs $7.50."

"Pretty good price for cigarettes," I said.

"Yeah, it's the lowest around here. I sell a lot."

"A carton would cost at least ten bucks in the States."

"Honey, that's not for a carton. Just one pack."

The road to Whitehorse had a lot of traffic control sections,
dust, and RV traffic. At one stop, I rode up to a flag-person, first in
line to go through a long section being re-graded. "Good," I
thought, "I won't have as much dust."

The girl stopping traffic said, "It will be a while."

I parked the bike in the middle of the road and sat down with
her under the big sky and among the black mountains. She was a
college student, making good money, but the work was pretty
boring.

The guide truck finally came and I followed him at a distance
to avoid the thick dust and the stones.

I stopped at the Information Centre in Whitehorse to ask about lodging. The girl at the desk suggested either the hostel in town or a campground run by the city. She never even mentioned any of the expensive hotels I later saw in town. I guess I no longer looked like the kind who would pay for a hotel room.

Excited by the prospect of sleeping inside, I went to the Fourth Avenue Residence. It was in a slightly seedy part of town and felt vaguely like a YMCA. The bulletin board had notices for inexpensive adventures and ads selling camping gear and outdoor equipment.

There were lots of different accommodations. Shared rooms with another person (a stranger). Private rooms with shared baths. Private rooms with private baths. Suites with kitchens. TV or no TV. I chose a private room with a shared bath, no TV, for $40.

There were cooking smells in the halls but it was clean and quiet. My room was in a little cluster of four rooms around a clean, modern bathroom. The furnishings were worn but serviceable. And it had a real bed. With sheets.

I unpacked my stuff and took a long shower. I lay on the bed and dozed, enjoying the quiet and the privacy of four walls. I could get used to sleeping inside again pretty quick.

I walked to the center of town for dinner and found a place that featured a large salad bar with lettuce, tomato, cucumber, sprouts, radish, carrot sticks, various pasta salads, and soup. Incredible luck! First a real bed and now a real salad!

Maybe I've been on the road a bit too long.

I woke in the middle of the night to muffled sounds from next door. "Oh, oh, oh, oh, oh . . ."

What the hell?

"Oh, oh, oh . . . ahh." Then silence.

Well, I thought, if that were me next door, it would have been a perfect night.

The morning ride was cold and I had to stop several times to warm up. At one of the stops, I saw a path leading through the shrubs to the tundra. I thought it might be a good place to see the permafrost so I followed it.

The builders of the original highway had lots of problems with the permafrost. When they scraped it away to prepare the roadbed, they found a deep mud-hole underneath that swallowed whole trucks and graders without a trace. Their solution was to build a corduroy road of logs placed next to one another on the permafrost. The roadbed was built on top of the logs. It left the permafrost undisturbed, but turned a traveler's insides into a milkshake.

The path merely went through the shrubs into an open clearing. Ugh. There were piles of shit and damp wads of toilet paper scattered around.

I thought I would be able to get breakfast on the way to Haines Junction, but there was nothing along this stretch of the road. It was a cold, hungry, two-hour ride as the landscape changed slowly from lowland river country to spectacular rocky peaks and incredibly blue glacial lakes.

Further down the road I rode off the highway to a small lake. Standing on the shore I felt as though I was on the dome of the earth, with everything falling away below me. Even the mountains, which seemed at shoulder level.

A car with New York plates passed me on a blind curve, crossing the double yellow line and forcing me to the inside. I caught up with the car later. It was stopped in the middle of the road with the doors wide open. As I pulled out to pass, the doors slammed shut and they raced away, throwing gravel that rattled on the fairing and my helmet. Is there nowhere one can go to avoid assholes?

I was in a roadside coffee shop trying to warm up when a huge Holland-America bus stopped. It was twice as long as a normal bus and was hinged in the middle to go around curves. The optional land tour for passengers on the Alaska Cruise. The Yukon Adventure Tour. I got away before anyone could ask me if I rode my motorcycle all the way from New York.

I passed another Holland-America bus a little further up the road. The passengers waved at me through the tinted glass windows.

23

Alaska

The worst section of the Alaska Highway was the no-man's-land between the Canadian and American customs stations. Frost heaves, potholes, washouts, gravel in the curves. At the American side, the officer said, "Welcome home."

Just over the border was a Last Chance truck stop. Last Chance to get gas. Last Chance to buy cigarettes—items that are typically much less expensive in the U.S. The signs on the Canadian side should read "First Chance to contribute to the Canadian government."

The most challenging stretch of my trip was the soft dirt road into the Tetlin Campground. The front wheel kept digging in and I almost lost it a few times. The trick, according to enduro riders, is to keep the power on and blast through the sandy stuff. I tried, but was too timid, I guess.

The campground was primitive. Pit toilets and no water. Only two other groups in the campground, an older couple in a truck-bed camper and two women in an elaborate wall tent.

The sun was still high when I finished setting up my tent at 9:15. It was still light at midnight and difficult to sleep, especially with the two women still talking about their relationships at home. They started up again early in the morning. When I left they were bickering about taking down the tent.

It was breakfast and decision time. Should I go to Fairbanks then head south on the scenic route past Denali National Park to Anchorage, then back down the Alaska Highway to Haines? Or should I just go to Delta Junction, the end of the Alaska Highway, and turn around?

The loop to Denali would add a lot of time to the trip. Fairbanks and Anchorage were big cities. It was a scenic route. Competition for campsites would be fierce.

I looked at the pictures in the brochures. Degrees of natural magnificence are hard to discern. Would more perfectly snow-capped mountains stir my soul even higher? I decided to turn around at Delta Junction.

I rode a short distance to Tok where I found a campground with flush toilets, hot showers, and campsites with beds of soft wood chips on which to pitch your tent. Because it was early, it was empty. And the motor home people typically continued on to Delta Junction where there were more tourist attractions, namely the End of the Alaska Highway and the Trans-Alaska Oil Pipeline. I had my tent set up by mid-morning.

The girl at the campground said the road to Delta Junction was the most boring part of the Alaska Highway.

"Maybe I should just skip it, then," I replied.

"Oh, no. You have to go to the end of the road after coming so far."

She was right. It was a symbolic gesture. Like standing up when you hear the national anthem.

There was another monument and a tourist information center at Delta Junction. I put my helmet at the base of the monument and took a picture. A gray-haired man in a green golfing shirt offered to take my picture. I said, "No, thanks. The helmet is enough."

I bought some postcards, sat in the sun writing them, and gave them to the clerk in the shop to mail.

It was the end of the road. From there on, I was headed home. I thought I should be elated, but I mostly felt relieved. Happily relieved, like finally finishing my income taxes. More "At last!" than "Hooray!"

That night I used my pickup truck restaurant rating system to find a place for dinner. The place I chose had a lot of pickups in front. Even better, most of them were filthy. There were no motor homes anywhere around.

The entry foyer had a glass-topped counter displaying cigarettes, chewing gum, and little cigars. It had a damp, stale beer and cigarette smell. Hank Williams wailed from a jukebox somewhere inside.

The dining room was dark with a haze of smoke under the overhead lights. There was a gray-bearded man wearing a cowboy hat sitting at a large round table with a fat woman and several other men wearing ball caps. I guess I found some oil pipeline guys at last. The people sitting alone were probably truckers. There were also some Indians drinking beer and talking story.

I ordered a beer in order to fit in and it came in a longneck bottle. No glass. The food was basic fried stuff, hamburgers that left my fingers feeling greasy even after I wiped them with a paper napkin.

Hey, no system is perfect.

24

Going Home

Sleeping on wood chips was as comfortable as a bed, and I woke refreshed but cold. It was only August but it already felt like fall. Time to head south.

I called the ferry that ran from Haines, Alaska, to Prince Rupert, Canada. The earliest I could get a reservation was in six days.

"Hell, I could ride back down the Alaska Highway in that time."

"But, you can stand-by in Haines. On a motorcycle you will probably get on with no trouble."

"Okay."

I made a reservation just in case and headed back down the Alaska Highway into Canada.

The Alaskan panhandle extends down the coast to Ketchikan, just north of Prince Rupert, where I was going on the ferry. But there are no roads into the area except through Canada to Haines, where the ferry begins.

So, for the first time on this trip, I retraced my steps. A sure sign that I was going home.

The Tetlin sandpit. The Last Chance. The minefield between the U.S. and Canada. The domed earth on the way to Kluane. Lunch at Kluane Lake, where I learned that the blue water was the result of glacial flour so fine that it stays in suspension in the water, changing its refractive index. Interesting, but I didn't need to know that. It was enough to see the blue glow in the cold gray drizzle that had begun.

I was passing RVs almost all day. None of them seemed to go the speed limit and staying behind them meant riding in a muddy mess of dirt and small stones. I had to wipe my face shield with the back of my glove every few seconds to clear off the mud so I could see. In the open, the clean rain and wind keeps the shield clear.

It began to rain seriously after lunch. I was wearing my longjohns, regular riding clothes, a sweater, and my leather jacket under my rainsuit. It was cold. My gloves were soaked and my fingers got so numb that I had trouble pulling the clutch and front brake levers.

I stopped at Haines Junction for coffee and to warm up after crossing Boulder Summit. I wasn't tired, but my senses seemed dulled, as though I were feeling things a few seconds after they happened.

If I kept going, I could get to Haines today. But the border closed at 5:00 and I might not make it. That meant camping overnight by the side of the road or in a primitive campground. In the rain.

The restaurant I had stopped in had a small motel attached. The Cozy Corner.

"How much is a room in the motel?"

"$60."

Only $45 US, I thought. "I'll take one."

The room was clean and spartan. It had a portable TV on a low stand and an armchair next to the bed. There was a tub and plenty of hot water. I soaked in it until the chill was replaced by a warm glow. That was worth the price of admission.

I went back to the restaurant and had a beer while I worked on my journal. It was early and the place was empty. I had lots of thoughts about the Alaska Highway now that I was about to turn off to go to Haines.

The trouble with the Highway is that it is all there is. There is no alternative. One road from Dawson Creek to Delta Junction.

No way to bail out. Like the Coast Highway, the ride eventually became a matter of simply getting to the end.

Don't get me wrong. It was beautiful. But when you have no choices, when you can't turn off and go someplace else, the experience changes. It's like being on a train traveling down a wonderfully scenic track. You move, but you are still in the same place, with the same people.

If it were challenging, a hard road, it might be different. But it was easy. Dusty, muddy, cold, slow, but easy. If a motor home or a double-length tour bus could do it, how hard can it be?

The road belongs to retired couples on their big adventure. I thought I would see hunters, trappers, fishermen, gold miners, lumberjacks, prospectors, and oil field workers. Instead, I saw mostly short, plump ladies in polyester pants taping uncooperative husbands with their video cameras. "Come on, George. Say something for the camera."

There were some bikes on the road. Mostly Gold Wings hauling trailers, some Harleys, a few BMWs, one or two enduros. But most of the traffic was motor homes and truck-bed campers driven by suspicious older people, a few pickups with caps over the bed and sleeping bags tossed inside, and even fewer small economy cars driven by college kids.

I was at the bitter end of the road. "Another beer?"

"Sure, why not?" I just finished the Alaska Highway.

Two women and two children came in and sat at a nearby table. I resumed writing after a quick glance. Then a small boy appeared at my elbow. "Is that your motorcycle outside?"

"Yes."

"What kind is it?"

"A BMW."

"Is it a racer?"

"No, it doesn't go that fast."

"Did you ride it from New York?"

"Yes."

"Where is New York?"

"Far away."

"Bobby, that's enough questions. I'm sorry. He loves motorcycles. We have been following you most of the day. We would catch up with you at a rest stop, then you took off and left us."

"It's okay. He has good questions."

Bobby sat down reluctantly and they ordered dinner. I did too. And I had another beer, since I was on a roll.

After dinner, I still had most of the beer. One of the women at the next table took the children to get ready for bed, leaving the other to finish her beer.

"Are you going to the ferry or down the Alaska Highway?" she asked.

She had a tight, small body and short dark hair. Her movements had the quiet efficiency of an athlete. "To the ferry, I rode up on the Highway."

"We're going to Skagway and plan to take the ferry back to Haines. It's just a short vacation trip with the kids. We live in Fairbanks."

"Maybe I'll see you in Haines. I have to wait there for the ferry."

"Your trip sounds great. How long have you been on the road?"

"More than two months."

"I took off one winter and worked as a ski instructor. It was great being free. You must be having fun."

"Yes," I said. I sensed the kind of tough independent spirit that attracts people to Alaska. "What do you do in Fairbanks?"

"My husband is a geologist with an oil company. I'm a geologist too, but the travel was too much. There were times we wouldn't see each other for months. I don't do field work anymore. But I miss it."

She introduced herself as Betsy. A solid, down-to-earth name, without the breeziness of "Liz" or the deliberate informality of "Beth." Her parents had given her "Elizabeth" but I knew she had chosen "Betsy". The name suited.

The next morning I woke with a dry mouth and a lumpy, tired feeling from drinking too much beer and sleeping in a warm, stuffy room.

There were several more people in the restaurant for breakfast.

A bicyclist was looking for a ride to the summit between Haines Junction and Haines. He was from Juneau and had taken the ferry to Skagway, planning to ride from Skagway around to Haines, then taking the ferry back to Juneau. The prospect of three more days going over the mountains in the cold and rain, with no services, had broken him, however.

"Yesterday was enough," he said to three men on a fishing trip who were headed to Haines. "If I can get to the summit, then I can coast down to Haines."

The three men were dressed in denim and flannel and heavy outdoor boots that laced above the ankles. They looked skeptically at the bicyclist, who was wearing a silly black and yellow spandex suit.

"Well," one of them said. "I don't know that we have enough room in the back for the bike."

"Yeah," said another. "He'd have to sit back there too. No room in the cab."

The bicyclist sat down dejectedly to wait for another prospect.

I sat with Betsy, her friend, and the two children. After breakfast, I showed Bobby the motorcycle and answered all his questions. They took some pictures of the children sitting on the seat of the motorcycle.

The road dried out as I began climbing toward the pass. Except for a short section of gravel, it was fast pavement. Above the tree line it was all gray. Sharp granite boulders below soft pillows of cloud. The summit was just below the clouds and I could reach up and stir the mist that pushed down in thin sheets, not quite rain but wet to the touch.

I passed a line of people going uphill on roller skis, thrusting their feet forward and pumping their arms back against their poles. Their colorful ski clothing was bright against the monochrome mountain.

I was back in The Ride. The cold disappeared even as I rode past banks of snow at the summit. I was astounded by the beauty of the area. My mind rang on after each vista, until the next pealed loudly, until it was like a springtime Sunday morning full of bells.

The road into Haines runs down a craggy valley of gray stone and gnarled pine trees. Eagles gather here every year to nest. It was a good place for eagles.

25

Haines

I went directly to the ferry terminal where I found a line of cars along the road waiting for the 3:00 northbound ferry. I parked in the nearly empty parking lot and went inside.

A sign above the ticket booth said, "Open at 1:00." I checked my watch. Twelve-thirty. I was hungry, but I might as well wait.

A ragged line of people stretched from the booth. "Are you waiting for the southbound ferry?"

"Yes, for standby tickets. Only an hour-and-a-half left."

"Doesn't it open at 1:00?"

"Yes, it's only 11:30." Ah, Alaska is one more time zone west.

There were already ten people in line, all four-wheelers. I went to lunch and walked through part of Haines. It was a pleasantly quiet seacoast town, so far unravaged by tourism.

The line had cleared out by the time I got back to the ferry terminal. I asked the ticket agent for a standby ticket for tonight's ferry.

She wrote it out then said, "Are you sure you want to do this? I think you will probably get on, but you have to get off the ferry at every stop, and most of the stops are in the middle of the night. And you may not get back on. That would leave you stranded for at least a day someplace you might not want to be."

I knew there had to be a catch. The thought of spending my Alaskan Cruise wrestling the bike on and off the ferry suddenly depressed me. I needed a break. And Haines was the best part of my trip, so far. I could go out to the glacier and mess around town.

"Why don't you stay in Haines? The State Fair is on right now."

That did it. I haven't been to a State Fair in years. "Okay. Forget the standby ticket."

I went to a grassy campground I saw on the way into town. "Just set up anywhere on the grass. There's plenty of room."

I put the tent up next to a picnic table under the trees. As I was finishing up an older man came over. "Are you sure you want to be here?" he said. "It's a lot warmer in the sun."

It was chilly under the trees. "Good idea," I said.

We picked up the tent and carried it into the sun. I staked it down. Then we hauled the picnic table over. I wanted a table since I expected to be spending a lot of time writing. I had five days to wait for the ferry.

"Did you ride up the Alaska Highway?"

"Yes."

"We did, too," he gestured toward two large Harley-Davidson motorcycles. They were touring machines, with the grimy patina of many miles of road. Two women in leather riding suits were sitting at a nearby picnic table and a large man was asleep on the grass.

"We're going on the ferry tonight. The campground people said we could hang around here until we have to line up. We camped here for five days. It's nice."

We walked back to their picnic table and I was introduced around. Harry, Alice, Jean, and Al, laying there on the grass. Two couples that had been riding together for more than 25 years.

Harry was a retired farmer, still farming, but retired. He was lean and agile, still looking like he could muscle big bags of seed into the planter. Alice was white-haired and matronly, even in her leathers. She was a passenger on this ride, but she usually rode her own bike. All of them had a solid Midwestern goodness that their biker disguise could not overcome. The kind of goodness that rushes to open doors for old ladies and cuts the neighbor's lawn while they are off on vacation. Decent people.

Jean was the oldest of the bunch but looked the youngest, probably because she dyed her hair. Al had a few medical problems. Seventy years old and a sugar diabetic. "This might be his last big ride," said Harry. "He had a serious problem because he stopped taking his pills. He had to go in the hospital, so we delayed our trip.

"As soon as they let him out, he wanted to leave. He's supposed to go for outpatient treatment, but he just took off. And when he got to feeling better, he stopped the pills again. I sure hope he makes it home."

Harry said all this understanding that Al was dying and needed to experience the road one last time. I almost understood. But would I be willing to ride alongside someone committing suicide?

Maybe. If he rode tall through the Frazier Valley and felt the hope in the desert. If he rode into the mountains and felt the air richen and cool. If he knew this part of the world was blue because he didn't look at it through tinted glass. If he didn't have to open a door to experience a place because he was always outside. If he didn't come out of the rain and cold because he couldn't anyway. If he forgot that he was 70 years old and a little shaky from the pills. If he laid down on the grass and slept when he was tired.

Sure, I'd do it. Even though they would say I helped kill him.

We spent the afternoon talking story. Al got up and we looked at the bikes, recalling each incident recorded in the dents and scratches. I got a list of good places to eat. They showed me a shortcut into town through a field behind the campground. We talked about the road and the rides. Nobody said the world was going to hell, or longed for the good old days. It was hard to be negative in Haines.

After they left, I went to dinner at a bakery they had recommended. It was just as they described, nearby and inexpensive. They gave me nearly a whole chicken, honey-fried. The huge portions made me consider cutting back to two meals a day.

At the campground after dinner, I walked over to see a couple on a Gold Wing, pulling a trailer. They were going on the morning ferry to Skagway and back down the Highway. They asked me to join them at their campfire, which I appreciated because the mosquitoes were starting to swarm. I could see black clouds of them against the sky. The smoke from the fire helped drive them away.

Jean was an English teacher at the Community College in Tacoma, Washington. Philip had just retired from the business administration office at the University of Puget Sound.

"How about that! I went to UPS in the '60s and just went back for a visit before coming up here."

"I'll bet you saw a lot of changes." He was tall and elegant, even in blue jeans, and had a mustache.

"Yes, and they are still after me for money to put up more buildings."

"Did you ride up the Alaska Highway?" asked Jean. She looked like a college English teacher about to retire. Gray, with a quiet resignation. Probably the result of trying to teach Shakespeare to college freshmen, a task we all know is pointless.

"Yes."

"Have you been riding long?"

"Over two months so far on this trip."

"Do you enjoy it?"

An interesting question from another motorcyclist. "Most of the time, but the motor home people bug me. How about you, do you enjoy it?"

"I guess so. This is our first long trip. I'm enjoying it, but I think I'm missing a lot. This adventure is a lot bigger than I am, but I take all I can handle."

"The Alaska Highway is a pretty serious undertaking for a first trip."

"Yes," said Philip. "It has been pretty rough. I had all kinds of problems. I dropped the bike a couple of times. Luckily, there were people around to help. Next time we should get something like yours, something a lot smaller and without a trailer."

Good. He was feeling the weight of the four extra cylinders and the two extra tires. "Motorcycles are minimalist vehicles. That's the freedom, just enough to get you where you want to go and no more. The least amount of stuff to worry about."

"Do you camp out all the time?"

"Most of the time. Every now and then I get a motel room because I think I need a break, but I always end up feeling I should have camped out. I guess it's because I only get cheap rooms."

They asked a lot of questions which I tried to answer honestly. They were curious, hesitant, but willing to try. We also talked about kids, taxes, public transportation, education, and suburbia. Easy things to complain about sitting around a campfire in Alaska. We talked so late that it got dark. My flashlight didn't work and I had to grope around in the tent to get ready for bed.

The sun striking the side of the tent woke me. It was comfortably warm, almost hot. Outside, the air had a thin, cold edge. All the other bikers were gone and I looked forward to a solitary day off the motorcycle.

After breakfast, I walked through the rest of downtown Haines. I stopped at the almost empty docks to feel the stunning whites and intense blues of seaside places in the sun. Most of the boats were out working the fall salmon run.

The air smelled like the edge of the Pacific, of salt and warming seaweed and potential. I grew up on an island in the middle of this ocean and remember standing on identical sea-smelling docks dreaming of Asia, Polynesia, and the Americas. The edge of the sea is an exciting place for dreamers.

I walked to the library where I sat in a comfortable chair and wrote in my journal. Time passed slowly, as it should on sunny days next to the sea, but it was over too soon.

That evening I went to a salmon bake run by the local Indian tribe. It was suspiciously tourist-oriented, but it was all-you-can-eat for $15, so I went. It turned out to be a laid-back fund-raiser staffed by enthusiastic volunteers.

I watched a young Indian dressed in a white T-shirt dip big orange salmon fillets in oil and grill them over a bed of red coals.

It was exceptional, with a sweet remembrance of the sea.

I had three pieces, along with a few roasted new potatoes and a beer, all included in the price. On my second trip I asked the cook for his secret recipe. "First we dip the fish in cottonseed oil. It keeps the fish from drying out and it doesn't add any flavor."

He basted the fish with a long handled brush. "Our secret sauce is made of butter, brown sugar, and lemon juice. We caught the fish today. That's the other secret. Fresh fish."

It began to rain during the night and I woke to a gentle drumming. The rain receded to a gray drizzle so I huddled under my rain hood and trudged to lunch, then on to the library. I wanted the comfort of a warm, dry place to wait and all there was at the campground was a small laundry room with no chairs. I spent the entire afternoon at the library reading magazines and browsing through books I want to read someday.

I bought an 1898 Lark Classic copy of *The Rubaiyat of Omar Khayyam* on the 25-cent book table. There was a drawing of a nude satyr playing a flute on the faded blue fabric cover of the little book. The corners were bent inward and frayed. The pages were brown and irregularly cut so they looked like a loosely stacked pile of papers.

The book was inscribed, Jessie Alice Haskins, March 23, 1900. I wondered if Omar spoke to Jessie on page 45?

A Book of Verses underneath the Bough,
A Jug of Wine, a Loaf of Bread—and Thou
Beside me singing in the Wilderness—
Oh, Wilderness were Paradise enow!

And did she take Omar's advice on page 59?

Ah, my Beloved, fill the Cup that clears
Today of past Regret and future Fears:
Tomorrow!—Why, Tomorrow I may be
Myself with Yesterday's Sev'n thousand Years.

She had marked the passages with a light pencil.

It rained again all night, sometimes heavily. I listened to it rushing on the tent and roaring in the trees. Stormy noises, accompanied by little splashes and gurgles of sea-bound water. The wet sounds were comforting despite having only a thin piece of fabric separating me from the cold misery. I could feel my mind and body mending after two months on the road.

Even with the rain, this was turning out to be a good stay. The light had a cool edge like the mountains, but it bore the weight of the sea. The sky had the splendor of a Shakespearean tragedy played on an endless stage. Brooding, intense, violent, crying, exulting, fanciful, laughing, the clouds performed all day.

Because the Fairgrounds were a little way out of town, I rode the motorcycle and parked next to what looked like an old delivery truck. It was painted several different colors, part with a brush and part with a spray can, as though someone was using up whatever paint was on hand. It looked like camouflage for a psychedelic forest. There was a stovepipe protruding from the roof and a thin stream of smoke rose from it.

Wild. A motor home even I could appreciate.

I walked around and peered in the passenger side window. I was looking right at a tall, skinny, gray-bearded leftover from the Flower Power era. He strode over and opened the door, which slid back on a track like a minivan side door. Warm air hovered in the entrance.

"Come in."

I clamored up a pair of steps into a small room that felt curiously like a rec room in a finished basement. If it were bigger it would certainly have had a pool table and a wet bar with a lighted Schlitz sign. Dark vinyl wood-grain paneling has that kind of ambience.

A bunk hung from one wall, suspended by chains like the sailors' racks in the enlisted quarters. There was a tiny stove attached to the stovepipe. A built-in table and two seats were across from the bed. A large red plastic cooler with a white top, and assorted cardboard boxes full of clothing completed the furnishings.

"Do you live in here?"

"I live in it most of the year. It's pretty good. I have four inches of insulation in the walls and roof. This year I'm going to insulate the floor and put in some carpet."

"Great. But what do you do?"

"I fish whenever I need the money. In the winter, I run a trap line. I used to work the fish processing plants, but it was bad."

What a life. Fish when you need the money and hang around the rest of the time in your motor home.

I went to the livestock exhibit first. There was a small collection of pet cows, sheep, and hogs in a large open-sided barn that smelled of manure and sawdust. Some small children were happily feeding the goats out of their outstretched hands. The poultry was in the Agricultural Hall. It's amazing how many kinds of chickens there are.

The photography contest in the Exhibit Hall was popular. Very artsy-crafty. Out-of-focus shots, some dramatically framed. Close-ups of doors and barn siding. Photographic clichés by high school students. Hey, it's how we all started.

Red, white, and blue ribbons decorated the winners of the quilting, basket-weaving, flower arranging, fruit preserves, and various vegetable contests. Some of the contestants were now badly-wilted.

Vendors selling everything from storm windows to all-in-one vegetable peelers pounced if you so much as hesitated at their booth. I learned that it was possible to heat a house made of Styrofoam blocks for less than $100 a year. And if you wax a car with Miracle Wax you can pour burning gasoline on it without harming the finish.

The town had moved the movie set from *White Fang*, a Disney film made in Haines, onto the fairgrounds. It consisted of a muddy Main Street, made up of a Saloon, General Store, Sheriff's Office and other frontier buildings. It was small, almost three-quarter scale. I wondered how they made the movie without making the actors seem like giants.

The rides were minimal. A toy train pulled by a disguised farm tractor, a merry-go-round, chairs suspended on chains whirling around a pole, and an air balloon in a tent for kids to bounce on. Thank God there was no creaking ferris wheel whose wooden spokes and worn iron fittings were sure to fail just when you were swinging at the top of the thing.

The food booths were a surprise. Pita pockets stuffed with king crab and avocado. Vegetarian pizza. Gourmet coffee or herb tea. Halibut and chips served in a cone of waxed paper. Mesquite barbecued chicken. And the classic Italian sausage and onions, hot dogs and sauerkraut, and curly French fries. I didn't see any cotton candy. Maybe it was by the coin toss and sharpshooter games.

More vendors were outside in tents. Bronze and silk stuff from Thailand, wool sweaters from Venezuela, custom-made knives with real antler handles. Pottery, woodcarvings, tie-dyed shirts.

An unusual feeling hung about the place. What was it? Monterey in the '60s? San Francisco's North Beach? Long, stringy hair, beards, braids. The uniform. Army surplus parkas, blue jeans, beads, long peasant skirts, clunky boots, backpacks. Laid back. "It's okay man, be cool."

I had found the last outpost of the love generation. Hippie guerrillas making their final stand against the yuppie invaders. Was that Joan Baez I heard ringing in the background like a small clear bell? Is it still the same sad yearning for compassion and tolerance? I hope so.

The entertainment was in a large open tent with long benches for seating. The singers performed on a raised stage surrounded by an array of black and chrome boxes. Tuck and Patti were well received by the small crowd. I thought Colleen Peterson was pretty good also. Folk music with a country edge. Or was it country music with a folk edge?

On the way out I saw a pair of BMW motorcycles like mine, but older versions, with European plates.

When I got back to the campground, I found two young bicyclists in the next campsite. They were from England, and had worked as contract cooks in Switzerland to earn money for their trip. One was headed home after happily completing his first bicycling adventure. The other was going on to Florida. He had earned enough to take a whole year off and travel.

The magic of Haines was everywhere. On the way to dinner I passed a natural food store. Flyers in the window advertised massages, acupuncture, and aromatherapy. After the bartender's shift was over at the Pioneer Inn, she sat down with a couple of guys to continue their conversation. At the Bamboo Restaurant there were vegetarian entrees on the menu. And at most of the places I ate in, come to think of it.

When I paid for dinner I discovered I had $20 more than I expected. The girl in the campground office must have given me the wrong change when I paid my bill. When I went back to the office, she said, "Don't worry about it."

My last day in Haines. I spent the morning trying to hike to a point where I could see the glacier better. There were signs at the trailhead warning about bears. After a couple of miles, all I had seen were woods, so I turned back. No glacier. No bears.

I lined up at the ferry terminal in the alley between two motor homes. The cold chill broke into a gray drizzle. The motor home ahead was running a generator that rattled in the damp air, driving away the comforting rain sounds.

The wait was a long 20 minutes while I resentfully imagined the motor home residents sitting in their warm, dry kitchens drinking coffee. Or maybe taking a nap on their king-sized bed. Or, toward the end of my wait, taking a leak in their private bathroom.

The gates finally opened and I was directed to park near the front of the staging area. It was still two hours before the ferry was supposed to depart.

I went into the terminal to take that leak and warm up.

26

The Inside Passage

I was the first to board the ferry. I slipped my way down the wet metal boarding ramp, locking my rear brake, as the boarding crew waved and shouted, "Hurry up! This way! Move it!"

I managed to make it down the ramp and to the stern of the ferry without dropping the bike, but it was tense going. I ended up behind two BMW motorcycles I had seen at the State Fair. A crewmember handed me a set of tie-downs. "Use your sidestand and keep it in gear," he shouted above the clanging din of the cars driving into the hold. "It's safer. Tie it down to this post and this pad-eye on the deck."

I tied the bike down as he suggested, but it still didn't look too secure, so I blocked the rear wheel using a pair of automobile wheel chocks and decided to check the bike after we got underway.

I went up to the passenger deck and watched the crew load the rest of the vehicles. Some of the motor homes were too large to negotiate the 90-degree turn into the hold and it took considerable backing, lurching, and yelling, "Okay. Stop! Go forward! Okay. Stop! Back up!"

Finally, the dock was empty and the mooring lines were slipped. The ship drifted imperceptibly away from the pier during that prayerful moment just after it releases its hold on land and before it surges forward under power.

Then the sea boiled under the stern and we were underway with a long, vibrating blast of the whistle. I felt the water moving under the hull and I longed to be on the bridge conning the ship.

Getting a ship underway, putting it back in its element, can be as joyful an experience as negotiating a set of curves on a motorcycle.

After we cleared the harbor, I tried to go below to check the motorcycle, but the vehicle deck was closed while the ship was underway. I had to wait until the next stop. So I checked out the ship instead. On the passenger deck there was a large observation lounge forward with rows of reclining seats that made it look like an extra-wide airline cabin. All the seats were occupied or piled with sleeping bags, jackets, and backpacks. Some people had spread out sleeping bags in corners and between the seats.

Just aft of the lounge was a bar on the port side and a cafeteria on the starboard side. Behind this was a large outside deck, partially covered with a canvas awning. There were cots, like those used for sunning at the beach, crowded under the awning. Somebody had set up a tent in the open area and it flapped and snapped in the strong onshore wind. All the cots were occupied.

There were private cabins in the deck below, with real beds and private baths, but they cost more and had to be reserved months in advance. Nothing for me down there.

I stood on the lee rail and watched the changing night sky, black and silver overhead, with a faint yellow reminder of the day on the western horizon. The moon reflected a glittering road to wonderful places.

In Juneau, I made sure the bike was okay and I got my sleeping bag, shaving kit, and towel. When I got back on the after-deck I found a recently-vacated cot and claimed it. Not bad, I was under a heat lamp that cut the chill.

A gray-haired woman bedded down next to me. She was wearing a housecoat and looked as though she was about to go to bed at the Holiday Inn. "This is a real adventure," she said. "I had to move from my other spot because of the drips."

A light rain had begun. "Why don't you go into the observation lounge?" I said. "There might be something in there."

"Oh, no. I want to give it a try outside."

Most of the people sleeping outside were young backpackers trying to avoid the cost of a cabin. Some disgruntled middle-aged people who couldn't get a cabin looked around, then went back into the observation lounge.

In the morning, my sleeping bag was damp and the decks had a slightly greasy coat of salt. The air was cold and brittle. The sun was shockingly bright.

We saw whales, announced by the watch officer, which produced an array of cameras and binoculars. The dark monsters surfaced, puffed, and dove, providing us with a few minutes entertainment.

A few small icebergs, as blue as the glaciers they had broken from, glowed in the black water like gemstones. Mountains surrounded us, striped with snow and graying in the distance.

I met the GS riders at the morning motorcycle check. They were Germans spending four months touring in Canada and the northwestern US.

Dirk looked German. He was fair, with blue eyes and short sandy hair. He wore a handlebar mustache that gave him a jovial, beer garden look. He had a large physical presence, and standing next to him in the dim hold felt like standing next to a padded wall. Thomas was darker, slimmer, and more intense. Hungrier. I sensed that he was the one that made most of the decisions.

They had done the Alaska Highway. The Klondike Highway to Dawson City. The Top of the World Highway into Alaska. Denali. The Valdez to Whittier Train. And now the Inside Passage. What a ride! My mind leapt at the possibilities.

Everyone I spoke with had a travel story. I met an American wearing a greasy-looking wool sweater. He had been traveling for years, through Asia and Hawaii. He went to Alaska to work on the fishing boats, but ended up working in the cannery when he missed the fleet. It was tough, smelly work, but the pay was good.

Now he was headed home, to a small town just south of Seattle. We worked through our connections. Bangkok, Chiang Mai, Singapore, Hong Kong, Tokyo, Kyoto, Honolulu. At the end of our talk he said he wasn't sure he wanted to settle down just yet. "Maybe I'll try Central America."

One acquires a grimy, travel-worn look after being on the road for a while. Part of it is a posture that waits patiently for opportunity. An attitude that endures discomfort without complaint. Open. Experiencing. Hopeless. The look causes pastel-clad tourists to shrink back in fear, or to stare from a distance as though they were observing lions at the zoo. The look also helps us connect with one another.

I met a slim girl with large blue eyes full of recognition and wonder. She had short dark-brown hair and a long neck like a fashion model. She had been traveling since January. Thailand, Malaysia, Singapore, Australia, and New Zealand. She flew back into Canada because it was cheaper. Went to Alaska. Now she was headed to Vancouver, then across the U.S. and down to South America. She was traveling with a guy who had been on the road for three years. "I'll keep going until the money runs out. That should be about February next year."

I fell asleep that night plotting to sell the house, the furniture, the lawnmowers and the cars.

Except for one person snoring loudly, there was peace on the afterdeck. It was comfortable under the heat lamps in the clean sea air. Much better than the moist staleness of the lounge.

In the morning there were gray panels of mist lying on the southern horizon while the sky above was clear and blue. The sun was yellow and warm.

Part 4
The Midwest

27

Canada II

We disembarked at Prince Rupert, through the bow doors of the ferry, down a short ramp, and onto solid ground. On the way out of town, I realized I hadn't experienced my sea legs, the rolling, loose-jointed walk one gets after a long period aboard ship.

I rode with the Germans to the campground at Burns Lake. They were fast and smooth. Thomas rode steadily. Dirk often slowed to take in a sight, then raced to catch up. I rode the middle ground.

The Germans carried their own food, so I stopped alone for lunch. We agreed to meet at a rest stop up the road. When I arrived at the rest stop, nobody was there. The rest stop overlooked a narrow canyon with a fish ladder next to some falls. There was a lot of activity near a bridge just above the falls. Maybe they were down there.

I rode down and parked on the bridge behind a large refrigerated trailer. There was a line of kids carrying white plastic buckets from the fish ladder to a large gray container.

Curious, I walked to the fish ladder. There were five pools in the ladder that allowed the salmon to rest between leaps to the next level. Each of the pools were full of salmon about 18 to 24 inches long.

Several Indian men were dipping for salmon with long-handled scoop nets about two feet in diameter. Each scoop brought up two or three salmon, which they dumped into the white plastic pails. The kids carried the fish to the container where colorfully-dressed Indian women packed them in ice. When the container was full, it was loaded into the trailer with a forklift truck.

I asked one of the men resting on the bridge how many trailers were filled each day. "Two or three," he said. "We call them and they bring another trailer and take away the full one."

An efficient, high volume operation. This is what the Northwest Indian fishing rights battle had been all about. Except it wasn't fishing. No baited hooks. No hoping for a strike. No bad days with nothing. It was more like looting than fishing.

I found the Germans at the next roadside pullout and we rode together to the campground, where we shared a site. I was set up in a few minutes and helped them with their elaborate cabin-style tent. It seemed too large for just two people.

After the tent was up, Thomas sat down at the picnic table with a can of Coke and a hip-pocket sized bottle of rum. "Rum and Coke," he said. "Want some?"

"No, thanks," I said.

Thomas drank a little Coke out of the can then filled it up with rum. He drank more and added rum until the drink was where he wanted it. Then he took out a cloth pouch of Bull Durham tobacco and rolled a cigarette, his fingers nimbly executing the complex task.

"We need to get beer," said Dirk. "We are Germans and need beer." When he said it, it was like the start of Octoberfest.

"I'm going into town for dinner," I said. "I'll get some on the way back." They were making their own dinner at the camp.

I was outside the liquor store strapping down a twelve-pack of beer when a young man wearing a white T-shirt and jeans came over. "Wow! I saw you guys when you came through town earlier," he said. "What kind of bikes are these?"

"BMW enduros." We must have looked like The Wild Ones about to invade the town. I was Marlon Brando.

"Did you just come back from Alaska on the ferry?"

"Yes." I guess we didn't look that sinister, after all, just travel-worn.

"Boy, I bet it was a great ride."

"Yes, it was."

We sat around the picnic table after dinner drinking beer and talking story. Dirk and Thomas were on their big trip. Dirk was a fireman and had two months off a year. He had taken an additional two-month unpaid leave of absence to take the trip. Thomas was a roofer and had quit his job to take the trip.

I was curious and asked, "Why do you have such a big tent? You could sleep four people in there."

"We started out with four people," said Thomas. "But one of us had a bad accident almost as soon as we arrived. He was passing a truck and got hammered down by the windblast.

"He was wearing an open faced helmet and his face got torn up badly. Also, his jacket rode up his waist and his stomach was ripped open. He had a leg fracture from an earlier accident and that broke completely."

"He was in the hospital for a week before they could send him home," said Dirk. "We waited with him in Toronto. Then, when we were going to leave, our other friend decided to go home also. He had lost his desire to travel. It was the fear."

"I can understand," I said. "An accident like that, especially with a riding partner, can shake you up pretty badly. Why did you keep going?"

"I wasn't sure," said Dirk. "But Thomas wanted to keep going."

Thomas opened another beer. "Look at it this way. I quit my job. We already shipped the bikes over here. We paid for the airfare. I had too much into the trip to just go home."

"But weren't you afraid after your friend got hurt?"

Dirk answered, "I was afraid. I would have gone home if Thomas hadn't wanted to keep going."

"I was afraid too," said Thomas. "I rode very carefully after that. I wear my helmet and my leather jacket all the time, and I keep it zipped up correctly."

A motorcyclist's clothing has several functions, the least of which is fashion. I looked at my helmet and leather jacket on the table. The helmet was stained by bugs and chipped by flying gravel. The jacket was worn white over the creases and had small white flecks over the chest where stones had bounced off of it. If I went down, would I be protected? I hoped so.

"Was it worth it?" I asked. "I mean, was it a good trip, after all?"

"It was good," said Thomas, with solid German conviction.

"I'm glad I kept going," said Dirk. "It was good."

We talked through the twelve-pack of beer. We revisited the Alaska Highway. I rode with them on the Top of the World Highway. I told them what to expect on the West Coast. We looked up nearby BMW motorcycle dealers in my club directory so they could get their bikes serviced.

The next morning I was ready to leave before the Germans were stirring. Now only two weeks away from home, I seemed to have a different sense of time and place, a sense of urgency I had not felt before. A need to ride driven by a combination of anticipation and road fatigue. I was anxious to get moving. I was no longer wandering. I was going home.

I left a note wishing the Germans good luck and headed into the slanting morning sun that made dusty shafts of yellow light in the dark woods and drew bright halos on the trees.

Going home. Peering into the lemon-tinted haze and black shadows as I descended through green meadowlands before turning south into the arid Frazer Valley. Approaching from the north, the valley was less impressive. Maybe, after having seen Alaska, I was just less-easily impressed. Or maybe it was just familiar. I was here only a few weeks ago. Or maybe my mind was already speeding ahead, toward home.

Going home. Making time.

On the way south, I passed 150 Mile House, 108 Mile House, 100 Mile House where I had stopped for dinner, 93 Mile House, and 70 Mile House. They were all little towns and I could never tell which house was the actual namesake.

I camped at Cache Creek, which should be Zero Mile House by my reckoning, in the same spot where I encountered the French-speaking couple on my way north.

28

The Rockies

The road forks at Cache Creek. I could ride east through the Canadian Rockies, or south into eastern Washington and across Idaho and Montana.

The Canadian Rockies are an exceptionally scenic area that has been invaded by Japanese tourists. I heard that signs in Banff are printed in Japanese and English. And that Japanese menus are available in all the restaurants. I saw what happened when the Japanese tourists started coming to Hawaii. The Japanese are big spenders. So we helped by making all the street signs and store windows in Japanese and English. Stores like Cartier, Gucchi, Tiffany, Ralph Lauren, and Banana Republic had opened. Most restaurants offered menus in Japanese. The most expensive restaurants served exquisite Japanese food.

Waikiki had become a glittering, money-lined village. A place with high ceilings, crystal chandeliers, and off-white furniture arranged on Turkish rugs. A Hawaiian steel guitar playing softly in the background. People wearing studiously casual designer clothes. Uniformed help. White stretch limousines with dark tinted windows. Flag-waving Japanese tour guides marching before platoons of tourists. It got to the point where you could hardly find a place to take a leak without some guy handing you a cloth towel over a conspicuous tip tray salted with dollar bills.

I headed south.

As soon as I turned off the Cariboo Highway onto Canadian Route 8, I knew I had made the right choice. The road went through a little town and over a one-lane bridge. Then it wound along a stream that tempted the dormant trout fisherman in me. Gray gravel washes, eddies and pools that had to have fish. How could fish not want to live in such beautiful places?

The landscape was high desert brown with strikingly green irrigated circles like gigantic polka dots. I saw a few of the irrigation systems at work, long pipes with sprinklers supported by wheels, rotating around wells. It seemed like a lot of trouble, but it must be worth it.

Climbing into the Cascades, there were orchards, then a series of lakes whose clarity perfectly reflected the sky and the surrounding evergreens. The color reminded me of a tourmaline ring we bought in Brazil. Emerald, more green than blue, more blue than green, a circle of intensity that distilled the essence of the landscape.

The summit was warm and I descended alongside another dream trout stream into Ossyoos, where I crossed the border.

The American side was . . . American. A different energy. A hungry, striving feeling. Not ugly or greedy. Just gently hurried. A sense of time running out. A line at McDonald's Drive-Thru. Everyone going 65 in a 55 zone. Pay-at-the-Pump. Gigantic farm machines working in fields so large they seemed like toys. Convenient ATMs. Trucks hauling double trailers. Drivers talking on cellular phones.

I rode east on State Route 20, going over the Kettle River Range at Sherman Pass. Just before the pass, the hillside was covered with dead trees. The bare trunks reached skyward from the black earth, their posture a reminder of their green vigor. Acid rain? When I got closer, I saw that there had been a forest fire, the branches charred black and shiny. Even the smell of the forest was burnt dry and dusty.

The summit was cold and heavily wooded, but it soon changed back into warming desert on the long slope into the Columbia River Valley.

I had a college friend who lived in Richland, in the center of the valley. He invited me home one Thanksgiving. My recollection of that visit was of a dusty suburb in the middle of a monotonous, level plain. An overwhelmingly empty place. Houses huddled together against unknown dangers, including the nearby Hanford Nuclear Power Facility. The valley hasn't changed much since then.

I stopped for the night at the Colville State Fairgrounds. The campground was behind a corral where livestock was kept during the Fair. The Fairgrounds were closed and the place had the sinister feeling of empty public spaces. As though the crowds had left malevolent ghosts behind. Spiritual graffiti.

I went to a semi-permanent camp next to the restrooms, thinking it was the manager's trailer. I walked past a mildewed awning under which was a picnic table covered with boxes of junk, a large collection of lawn chairs, roughly stacked, and several gas barbecue grills in various states of repair. Behind the trailer, a small group of men dressed in denim overalls and flannel shirts were sitting around a cold fire pit. They looked threateningly at me when I approached, as though I were disturbing some very private ritual.

"Can I get a campsite?" I asked.

There was a moment of silence, as though they were deciding whether to answer. I started to get nervous.

Finally one of them said, "Set up anyplace. Somebody will be around to collect in the morning."

Oh, they were not the managers. They turned back to their ritual and I left quietly.

Later that evening, two girls came in and set up their tent using the headlights of their car to see. I didn't sleep well, feeling the heavy presence of the empty fairgrounds.

I was out of there early. Nobody had come by to collect and I didn't want to hang around. Breakfast cost $1.29 and I left a 50-cent tip. Back in the USA.

On the way out of the restaurant, I met a guy and his young son wearing matching T-shirts. Blue, with the BMW logo and the "Legendary Motorcycles of Germany" slogan across the front. He said he rode a last edition RS, but was in his car for this trip because of the family.

He suggested a shortcut to US 2 that would avoid the construction on Route 20. "Just go south on 395 until you hit the Esso station at Loon Lake. They will give you a map showing you how to do it from there."

I rode to the Esso station and was given a hand-drawn map with the directions marked in blue. I was headed east on US 2 shortly afterward. US 2 runs across the northern states just below the Canadian border, from Puget Sound to Lake Michigan. Its importance has been diminished by Interstates 90 and 94, which run cross-country just to the south. Still, the road was busy and continually populated with farms and businesses. I saw no signs of abandonment. No vacant storefronts and decaying structures. The towns were small, but had healthy downtowns and pleasant main streets.

Sandwiches here are either sold alone, meaning without extras, or "In a basket," meaning with fries and cole slaw.

Ordering lunch was an adventure. "I'd like an egg salad sandwich and french fries."

"In a basket?"

"A plate is okay."

"It comes on a plate."

"Good."

"Do you want cole slaw?"

"What?"

"Do you want cole slaw or a side of fries?"

"I'd like an egg salad sandwich and french fries."

"In a basket?"

This was getting repetitious. "Okay. However you serve it."

"Okay. Egg salad in a basket."

"With fries."

"Okay."

I waited expectantly for my lunch basket. It came on a plate with a mound of fries and a tiny paper cup of cole slaw. Like the waitress said, no basket.

At the end of the day I was near the entrance to Glacier National Park with no alternative but to stay at the KOA Campground. It was crowded, expensive, and infested with motor homes.

I got one of the last tent sites inside the grounds. Otherwise I would have had to use the overflow area, which was a strip of mowed grass next to the highway. It was free, but you had to pay the regular price to use the campground facilities. There were already a few motor homes parked in the overflow area.

My site was next to a shiny full-size 4x4 truck hauling a late-model, chrome-laden, big-twin Harley. Everything spotless. Mint. I was probably looking at $50,000 in machinery. It glittered above me as I set up my tent.

The driver of the Harley rig came over as I was finishing up. "Did you ride that bike all the way from New York?" he asked.

"Yeah. I'm on my way back from Alaska."

"We live in Los Angeles. We're on vacation and I brought the bike in case we wanted to do some riding. But I don't think I would want to ride it this far."

He looked at my campsite.

"Where do you put all your stuff?"

I gestured at the tent. "That's all I got."

"I'd never make it this far with what I can carry on the bike. Forget Alaska."

I put the conversation back on more familiar territory for him by commenting, "Nice bike."

"Thanks," he replied. Then he recited all the statistics. Year, model, displacement, modifications—as though he were writing an ad to sell the machine. Cruiser conversations are often like that. Intensely mechanical. Of course, if I had been riding a Harley myself, the recitation of statistics would have been unnecessary.

We debated the advantages of belt drive vs. chain drive. A belt is cleaner and quieter, but a chain looks cooler, and appearance is critical, since American motorcycles and hot rods are more than transportation. They are an example of a genuine American folk art, practiced by unlikely, but genuine, artists.

The campground weekly barbecue was that night and I decided to give it a try. The food was served in a large, open-sided shelter filled with wooden picnic tables. Two choices. Chicken or steak.

I found an empty table, ordered the chicken, and was settling down with my journal when two couples sat at the other end of the table. They were dressed in the kind of crisp, resort-style clothing one finds in the Lands' End catalog. They seemed not to notice my presence.

One of the women looked at the menu and said, "I guess we all will have the chicken."

"Speak for yourself," said the other woman. The two men sat quietly alert. Waiting.

"We just ran out of chicken," said the waitress, defusing the situation.

They ordered steak instead. Medium rare. Medium. Medium well. Medium well, done more well than medium, no red meat, a little pink is okay.

After the waitress left, they launched into a critique of the campground, going over every detail from the restrooms to the playground areas. They spent a lot of time discussing hookups for water, electricity, and cable TV, as well as the location of the pump-out station. Inspectors for KOA? RV magazine critics?

"You know, this is the future of family vacation travel," said the chicken lady. "Cruise America is the best idea so far. The owners get to recover some of their investment and still use their RV whenever they want. And the people who can't afford to buy, or don't want the hassle of ownership, can rent an RV whenever they want."

So that's what that "Cruise America" sign across all those RV windshields meant!

"The industry is doing a lot of PR, getting campgrounds to offer more services and communities to cooperate with better parking, pump-outs, and so on."

Another man strode up to the table. He looked like the kind of person you see making deals over lunch at fancy restaurants, except he wasn't wearing an Armani suit.

He turned to me and said, "Hello, how are you? Are you enjoying your trip?" His questions had the kind of cordial insincerity that headwaiters and hostesses cultivate.

I automatically answered, "Fine, thanks," although I was starting to feel hostile.

Formalities aside, he turned to the group to work the sale. The guy was good. He dressed casually, like his customers, except his clothes were by Ralph Lauren, conveying class and authority. He was smooth, attentive, concerned, asking more questions than speaking himself, making encouraging comments at the right moments. He played on their insecurity and greed.

I left after I finished eating. I knew by the time Ralph Lauren was done, the Lands Enders would be believers, ready to see that every suburban house in the country had a motor home in the driveway.

I slept poorly. Somebody was snoring loudly all night. Probably the guy with the Harley on his truck.

29

The Great Plains

In the morning, I followed US 2 south to avoid the lumbering RVs on the scenic drive through the park. Beyond the last mountain pass, the road quickly descended into the Great Plains. Towering dark green trees shrank into yellow wheat fields, the horizon falling below my shoulders, then my knees, until I rode on the apex of the domed plains. Clear mountain air ripened into an agricultural haze that slowed, but could not stop the endless view. Like my vision, the wind blew unobstructed, constantly seeking something over the horizon.

Then tallgrass prairie, silvery green and so much like the ocean that I thought my hand would be wet if I touched it. It moved like the wind-driven swells on the ocean after a storm. Once this whole place was covered with tallgrass, a rich inland sea teeming with life. We have been killing it, draining it to make thousand-acre farms.

I was moving fast. Cattle ranches with fences reaching over the horizon like threads in a gigantic spider's web. Grain, looking like a yellow sunset at sea. A river valley and oddly confining trees. Back to cattle in a dusty hilly region. A desolate Indian reservation. Isolated farms, their distant silos rising like phallic symbols. The other buildings a smear on the horizon. Small towns pressed down by the heavy sky, no buildings more than a story tall. Grain elevators alongside railroad tracks, looking like Lionel model train settings.

I started spacing out somewhere near Saco, Montana. My mind lost its focus. Random thoughts drifted in and out as I rode along. Riding blindly, on autopilot. It was the scale of the place. Too big. Too empty. I sought shelter inside my head.

I jerked out of it, suddenly afraid. I had to get off the road. O'Brien's Motel was off to the left with a bar and restaurant in front.

The motel was a long, low building at a right angle to the highway. There were only a half dozen rooms, their doors opening directly to the parking space outside.

I couldn't find the office so I went into the bar. "Where is the motel office?" I asked.

"This is it," answered the kid behind the bar. "Want to look at a room?"

"How much?"

"Eighteen bucks."

I took the key he offered. The furnishings were slightly worn, but it was clean and had TV and a window air-conditioning unit. Not having to put up the tent in the wind was worth two or three dollars.

I took a shower then went back to the bar. A gray-haired couple were nursing their beers in a booth. Two young men played at the pool table, the clicking balls echoing in the room.

I sat down at the bar and ordered a beer. "Anything going on in town?" I asked the bartender.

"No, not around here. I go to Montana State in Bozeman. I can't wait to get back there so I can have a social life."

"What are you studying?"

"I don't know what I'm going to major in yet. I like playing music, but I can't see myself majoring in it."

"Why not?"

"It's pretty hard to make a living as a musician. Plus, you don't need a college degree to play the kind of music I like."

"Jazz?"

"No, mostly rock-and-roll."

"Well, what subjects do you like?"

"I guess I'm not really interested in college. I'm only going to get out of here. This is a pretty deadly place."

I could feel his dissatisfaction. I wanted to tell him to just dump everything and join a band. Play for food. Do charity gigs for the exposure. Go to New York and play on a subway platform.

But I knew the trap. The golden bait in the center. The bars made of high-grade anxiety. What the hell, I had spent most of my life in that cage. And I might be headed right back into it.

So I just said, "Then you better pick something like engineering or science. Maybe math. Lots of musicians are good at math. You can get a job as a computer programmer."

Eight-thirty and the sky was still light. There was a soft purple haze on the low hills. The grain elevator was a hulking black menace across the road. Clouds of mosquitoes hummed in the lee of the building.

The next morning was cold. The road was wet in spots where it had rained the night before. I felt I was riding on the edge of a rainstorm, in the moist stillness just before the rain. The sky was clearing to the northeast, but overhead was piled with heavy gray clouds resting on ominous black bases.

The day stayed cold. The sky changed continually as I chased a patch of blue on the eastern horizon. Clouds massed then danced away, displaying more shades of gray than an Ansel Adams print.

I found another $20 motel in Minot, North Dakota. These places were tired but clean, and it sure beat setting up a tent in the wind and rain.

I don't know what it was. Road fatigue? The end in sight? The vast monotony of the Midwest? Anyway, I was suddenly anxious to get home. I looked at my maps, trying to plot the fastest route. If I followed US 2 all the way to the top of Lake Michigan, then went across Canada, around Georgian Bay, and back into the U.S. in Buffalo, I could do it in four days, maybe three if I pushed hard.

But I had to visit my old friend Jerry in Rochester, Minnesota. He was expecting me and had already called Margaret to find out where I was. To see him, I had to go much farther south, probably adding another two days to the trip.

Then I was ashamed that I would even consider not seeing Jerry just to save a couple of days. I needed to save The Ride, to hold onto every mile.

In the morning I turned south, left US 2, and headed through intensive farm country toward Rochester, Minnesota. There were little towns quietly located off the highway every 20 miles or so.

It took me a while to figure this out. I would come to what was supposed to be a town, and I would find only a grain elevator, agricultural equipment store, or gas station. At first I thought, "Well, everybody must live on their farms."

Then I took a side road and found a small town gathered around a square. It felt quaint and comfortable. The kind of place Norman Rockwell might have painted. The kind of place where not much happens, but where you can walk everywhere and know everyone. America, just a little way off the main highway.

After that, I left the highway whenever I needed a break.

The countryside changed from yellow wheat and occasional sunflower fields, to green pasture, corn, soybeans, and lots more sunflowers. And lots more bugs that splattered on my face shield and turned my jacket into a furry mess.

All day it rained nearby. The rain gathered like flocks of birds foraging over the fields. Gray rainbirds drenched the fields a mile away. I never got caught, although I rode through the aftermath of a storm and my legs got wet from the spray.

I stopped for the night at a Super 8 Motel. It was modern, comfortable, and convenient. I justified it by noting that there were no campgrounds nearby and the price was good, only $35. All this was true, but I could have stopped earlier or taken a detour to a campground. Was the ride slipping away?

Things had changed. I was headed home. Picking the fastest route. Riding long hours. Not wanting to take the time to set up and take down the tent.

I still heard the landscape singing, but its rhythm had changed from a ballad to a dance. Going home, surely a different person for all that I had seen and done. Like that last week at college before going home for the summer. Writing papers. Anxious to leave. Taking exams. Already packed up. Wondering if things had changed, if I had changed?

All morning there was a strong south wind, which forced me to ride with the bike heeled over to the right, as though I were constantly turning. I learned to anticipate the windbreaks, straightening up in the lee of trees, buildings, and berms to avoid swerving right when the wind dropped. Even the hills and distant trees shaped the wind, making invisible rivers and fast-breaking waves in the hazy air.

The wind carried smells from far over the horizon. The razor-sharp smell of hogs. The damp, salty smell of cattle. The brown smell of freshly turned fields.

The scent of serious agriculture.

30

Rochester, Minnesota

I had attended a public school program called English Standard that had been developed to counteract pidgin English, the exotic street language of Hawaii.

Pidgin evolved because people needed to talk to one another. Hawaiians to Americans to Japanese to Portuguese to Chinese to Filipinos. Together on a small island, they made a language that helped them buy and sell, work and play, fight, love, and marry. It worked on the plantation.

But Hawaii was annexed. The plantations were mechanized and the island economy grew. Mainland connections increased. And, like every other group of immigrants that came to America, everyone realized good English would be a key to their success.

English Standard was the choice for upwardly-mobile local families who couldn't send their kids to Punahou, the private school for haole (white) kids. To get into the English Standard program, you had to pass a test that showed you could speak proper English. I passed the test in kindergarten, so I spoke the exclusive language of the haole upper class in school, while I played with the kids in our working class neighborhood in a language that blended our Polynesian, Asian, and European cultures.

It was a schizophrenic existence and I never felt part of either group. The color of my skin excluded me from one and the color of my language kept me at arm's length of the other. So I spent much of my pre-pubescent time on private eccentricities like raising homing pigeons, building simple electronics projects out of

Popular Electronics magazine, trying to develop photographs in a closet darkroom, and reading.

I had what might charitably be called a difficult adolescence. In high school my overflowing hormones mixed with gasoline to create a high-octane craziness. I spent a lot of nights trying to fulfill my sex drive in the back seat of a '56 Ford. During the day I fooled around with the engine and chassis of the '56. Late nights were spent aimlessly cruising through drive-ins and staging spontaneous drag races at Sandy Beach.

Most of my high school classmates were smart and ambitious. Nice kids, despite all that. They studied hard, and went to pep rallies and socials. The guys were going to be engineers or doctors, and the girls wanted to be schoolteachers or doctor's wives. My high school ambitions were simpler. I wanted to get laid and do the quarter-mile under twelve seconds.

Okay. I screwed up in high school and have been struggling since then to get over it. But I am not going to tell you that I learned from my mistakes and am a better person as a result. I didn't, and I'm not. They were just mistakes. Dumb, juvenile mistakes. My mistakes. Many of my adolescent memories are painful. I am sorry if I hurt anyone other than myself, and I probably did, I'm sorry.

What was it about the great plains that had caused my mind to recede to ancient regretful places? Was it the rain? The endlessly level landscape? The recollection of dark, melancholy nights at sea? The Gothic loneliness?

Whatever. Now my memories had flared like an arthritic joint. Older remedies were not available to me here on the open plains, such as hiding in my private office and center entrance colonial. Or becoming a workaholic to prove it wasn't me that screwed up. Or distracting myself with endless business meetings and a lifetime of TV. Or drinking enough to numb, but not enough to kill those persistent adolescent memories.

I guess that sooner or later we must learn to live with our package of memories and dreams. So, in the vast emptiness of the Midwest, I remembered my old friend Jerry and all the turmoil surrounding period of my life. And I thought, "What the hell, let it go."

To be fair, I did learn something in high school besides how to unhook a bra and rebuild a flathead Ford. I had joined the Camera Club and had gotten access to the school darkroom. I still remember expectantly watching my first enlargement appear on a sheet of paper immersed in Dektol. And, to this day, that miracle of revelation still excites me.

I started taking pictures. I learned to judge light better than a light meter. I started "seeing" pictures. True, they were adolescent pictures, but I was learning. I made 16x20 prints of a scene in Nuuanu Valley in the style of Ansel Adams. I went to Tantalus at night and took pictures of Honolulu city lights while couples necked in nearby cars. I tried to talk girls into posing nude and settled for bathing suits.

I went to the University of Hawaii in the fall. Yes, they let me in after I made up a required course in summer school. Their standards weren't really that low. My father was on the faculty of the University.

I dropped out in the second semester. I guess I couldn't reconcile English, Sociology, and College Algebra classes with the reality of living on an island where career opportunities were mostly agricultural, like picking pineapple. Or connected to tourism, like waiting tables.

The classes were all given in large, impersonal lecture halls filled with earnest students who really believed that mastering Ohm's Law was their ticket to the good life. It was hard. I tried, I stood in long lines, clutching odd scraps of paper, to register for courses. I bought the books and sat through lectures where professors droned incomprehensibly to the blackboard. I went to the library to study at large tables littered with books and the heads of sleeping students finally overcome by boredom.

And everywhere outside was Hawaii. The scent of pikake. Dazzling white beaches fringing impossibly blue water. Soft green textures on the hillsides. And light. Tropical light that highlighted every dazzling wave and made mystery shadows in the forest. Light that warmed and painted every face with exotic color.

When I finally couldn't take it anymore, I stopped going to classes and started looking for a job. For someone with my skills, the job market was limited. I could have gone back to pumping gas and doing lube jobs. The pineapple cannery was also gearing up for the summer season. And there were jobs in Waikiki, watering grass, parking cars, or selling souvenirs to the tourists.

Pretty poor choices. But I figured that even if I had a liberal arts degree from the UH, the choices would have been the same.

Then I got lucky and found a job working from 10:00 at night to 6:00 in the morning in a photography lab as an apprentice to a master printer. We had to develop all the pictures that were taken during the day so that they could be delivered the following morning. They were mainly shots of tourists with Hawaiian models dressed in hula costumes taken at hotel luaus or scenic vistas. Or of group tours wearing their complementary leis with Diamond Head in the background. Or of visiting congressmen shaking hands with local notables. Or group pictures of reunions and teahouse parties. The occasional wedding.

I learned processing from Tad. He was a small man with a precise manner, much like the cameras he loved. He worked in an intensely efficient fashion, his equipment always arranged to minimize wasted motion. His interest in photography was more technical than artistic, which was good for me since he could not tolerate sloppy work, even on silly pictures of tourists. "Do it right," he insisted.

So I learned the trade. Mixing chemicals, developing roll and sheet film, making prints, drying, and finishing. In a short time, I was doing production work. With two people working, we often finished early. Then we would experiment with chemicals and film. Push processing to see how fast we could make Tri-X or developing Panatomic-X in diluted developer to see how fine we could get the grain.

I believed that if I mastered photography, I could always pick up a camera and make a living. So I tried to learn everything. I asked for shooting assignments and started working evening luaus and group picture assignments with Walt Pollak, the big, red-faced owner of the business.

Walt loved equipment. He used a Linhof Super-Technica with a super-wide lens that looked like a Coke bottle. He had a Hasselblad that was always being sent back for service so he bought a second Hasselblad so that he would always have at least one working. He had more Leica equipment than I have ever seen since. He put CB radios on the fleet of Hillmans we used as company cars, so we could communicate. He was continually tinkering, perfecting his equipment.

A lot of people love photography only for the technological precision of its instruments. You know them. They always buy the latest cameras, marveling at the amazing glassy expanse of an f/1 lens or the unbelievable whispered click of a shutter blinking at 1/2000 of a second. Too often, the pictures these people take are mediocre. Some never take pictures, satisfied with the potential their cameras represent.

But Walt was a good photographer. Not an artist, but a craftsman who could be counted on to take a good picture under any circumstances. We had been making pictures to sell on the street, and that meant we had to take better pictures than the typical tourist in Waikiki. Pictures the typical amateur couldn't make.

I remember going with Walt to a teahouse before a shoot and setting up dozens of small flash units so that we could take a group picture with everyone at the tables. I have never since seen a more evenly illuminated flash picture. Everybody was easily recognizable in the big 11x14 print.

Walt once sent me to the Diamond Head Lookout, where I had spent many evenings watching submarine races with girlfriends. I had a 500mm lens mounted on a Leica. My job was to shoot the boats crossing the finish line of the Trans-Pacific Yacht Race, then use the radio to alert the office that the boats would soon be arriving at the Kewalo Yacht Basin. It was an impressive demonstration of technology for the time. I got some great night shots of boats illuminated by searchlights from the shore.

Jerry came to work for Walt in that summer of discovery. He had finished high school in Janesville, Wisconsin, and had decided to come to Hawaii. Pale, quiet, and self-deprecating, he did-n't seem like an adventurer. And he definitely wasn't a tourist. Just a regular guy on a ride, testing his limits.

Jerry grew up in this vast place I was passing through. With its relentlessly hard wind and wheat fields that mimic the ocean but have no beaches, so hopelessly flat and endlessly fertile. Eating meat and potatoes. And suffering fierce unknown winters.

It wasn't hard to figure out why Jerry wanted to get out.

Hawaii has a narcotic quality that immobilizes many who live there. As a kid, I never thought beyond the line of surf that sur-rounded the islands. I could not imagine living in a place without tradewinds, sandy beaches with the Koolau Mountains behind, and the scent of plumeria everywhere. Without eating saimin, laulau, poi, makezushi, and adobo. Without endless summer.

I was never going to leave Hawaii.

But meeting Jerry changed everything. He was my age. He had broken out. He had no history. He was free. Maybe it *was* possible to go away and start over.

Jerry fit well into the group at Walt's. Like the rest of us, he loved taking pictures, working in the darkroom, and playing with cameras. He was a competent photographer. He never com-plained and joined in all our activities.

After his adventure in Hawaii, Jerry stayed in photography. He became a photojournalist and carved out a respectable career with the Gannett newspapers, moving to larger and larger papers around the country. His last job was with the Rochester, Minne-sota, paper.

Sometimes, when we heard from him at Christmas, I was a lit-tle envious. There I was, pushing paper across a desk, while he was outside making pictures. It would be great to see him again.

Jerry's house was in a quiet residential district. He was stand-ing in the driveway when I arrived. He was still slim, with the same quietly expectant posture. His hair was gray and thinning. There were deep wrinkles on his face, like a face that had been peering into the sun too long.

I recognized him instantly and we shared that awkward moment that bridged the past and the present. Until we suddenly had to talk.

"How are you?"

"Good."

"How was the trip?"

"Fine."

Until we got to that place that mattered most to us. To that place we left off 30 years ago.

"What about you? How are things going?"

"They closed the photo lab at the paper and I was laid off. Everything is digital today. They process the film in a minilab, scan the negative, and do the layout on the computer. No prints."

"What are you going to do?" I couldn't imagine Jerry without a camera.

"I knew it was coming so I set up here at home. I get the negatives from the paper and make prints for people that want copies. I do custom printing. Weddings. Parties. That kind of stuff. I'm going to set up a studio in the garage. I was just doing some measurements. Make it a real business."

"Can't you get a job with another newspaper?"

"I guess so. But we don't want to move. Diane has a good job and we have family here. Anyway, all the papers, even the small ones, will be going digital soon. We are obsolete, Notch."

We went inside and Jerry showed me his lab.

"Remember this piece of equipment?" he asked. He had his hand on an old Leitz Focomat, a constant-focus enlarger that used screw-mount Leica lenses. It had a system that kept the image in focus as the size was adjusted. I remembered it was very quick and convenient to use.

"When the lab closed, they sold all the equipment. I got a lot of stuff really cheap. Good stuff. Like this enlarger."

"It must be 40 years old. My father had one when I was a kid."

"It still works fine. I use it a lot."

We are obsolete, but we still work fine. Like the old rotary phone in the basement. I guess Jerry made sense. Why abandon something that has always worked so well?

Jerry's parents joined us for dinner, along with his son Jim and daughter Julie. Diane barbecued ribs, and made corn-on-the-cob and potato salad. We ate on the deck. Then we sat in the long Midwestern afternoon and talked story.

Jerry's mother was a slim, pleasant-looking lady. She was dressed in the simple timeless style that elderly women adopt after they give up trying to be fashionable. She wore a black hairnet over her white hair.

"You know," she said. "I used to ride on a Harley '74 Army Edition back in the '40s."

I was surprised, but she knew what she was talking about.

"We used to ride out West. We went up Pike's Peak when it was all dirt roads. Of course, most of the roads were dirt back then. My, it used to be such fun. Today it's all boring interstate."

Our conversation moved as naturally as our breath from topic to topic. "You know, I have a picture of you boys in my scrapbook. I was just looking at it today. It was taken in Hawaii in 1959. Jerry sent it to us."

Jerry's father was dressed in a sport shirt and unfaded blue jeans turned up at the cuffs. He wore black, Army issue shoes. He had the odd, mismatched look of someone who refused to sacrifice function for fashion. For him, dressing up meant wearing newer, not more special, clothes. A resolutely practical man. He even drove a Chevy truck instead of the regulation Buick.

"Yes," he said. "We've been married 52 years. But don't you feel sorry for me."

Julie sat quietly, listening to the old folks talk. Jim also sat quietly, but he had a sullen energy that deflected all conversation in his direction. He left after eating to go trapshooting with his girlfriend. Jim was a tough case. He had gotten into trouble and done some jail time. Drugs, I think. He got into a fistfight with Jerry, hurting Jerry badly, and was estranged for a while. I was glad to see that he was back at home. It wasn't easy for anyone in the family, including Jim. But I was glad that their home was the kind of place where, "when you have to go there, they have to take you in." I was glad that everyone in that family knew that home was something you somehow haven't to deserve.

You know. Robert Frost. "The Death of the Hired Man." In these great, forgiving, plains. In the Heartland of America.

31

Rochester, New York

If you look at a map, you will see that Lake Michigan sits across a straight line connecting the two Rochesters. The land routes go either around the north end of the lake, or south through Chicago and Cleveland. An extra day, either way. If I took the ferry across the middle of the lake from Wisconsin to Michigan, however, it would be almost a straight shot home.

I left early so that I could get as close as possible to the ferry before stopping for the night. I wanted to make the morning crossing on the following day.

The air was very hazy, with a yellow-gray band obscuring the horizon. It was level, intensely agricultural land. Mostly corn and soybeans. Dairy and hogs. Always one or two clusters of farm buildings off in the distance. Silos. Towns closer together. Bigger.

The further east I traveled, the greener the landscape became. The occasional tree became a windrow, then a stand, then woods. Never enough to be a forest, though. And they were mostly hardwoods. Oak, maple, locust, willow, ash. Only a few ornamental evergreens. The opposite of the predominant evergreens on the West Coast. There was an early yellowing maple announcing the coming of fall.

I crossed the Mississippi again, going home.

After spending the night in Oshkosh, I arrived at the ferry an hour early and backed into a parking space next to a big Harley.

The riders were sitting on a small grassy strip between the parking area and the road.

"Get your ticket inside," the man called out. "You can leave the bike there."

I bought my ticket and joined the Harley riders on the lawn.

"I'm Floyd and this is my woman, Jean." Both of them were wearing black leather jackets. Jean's had fringes dangling from the sleeves.

"Hi. I'm Notch."

"Where have you been?"

"I'm on my way back from Alaska."

"Wow! We're on our way home too. But it was just a three-day trip in Minnesota."

They were eager to hear about the ride, so I told them about the road, the camping, and the ferry. We talked as though they were going there soon, as though these were things they needed to know before they left. We never spoke of the beauty and mystery one would encounter along the way. They already understood all that.

"Sure, you could do it on a Harley if you don't mind it getting a little dirty."

"I fix appliances for a living. I might be able to get enough time off," said Floyd. "It's no problem for Jean since she's unemployed right now."

"I'm an accountant," said Jean. "There aren't a lot of jobs around."

"Then you might as well go to Alaska. Since you are free."

We were waiting for the ferry to complete refueling when a woman riding a BMW R100RT touring motorcycle came in. Her legs were so short she couldn't get both toes down at the same time. She stopped and wobbled the bike onto the side-stand.

"Hi. I need to get my ticket. I hope I'm not too late." She rushed into the office.

She came back quickly, clutching her ticket. The coal truck refueling the ferry had gotten stuck on the boarding ramp and there would be a delay.

"I just made it. I don't know what I would do if I missed the ferry. I have to get to Detroit by tomorrow."

"It would be a long ride," said Floyd. "I'm Floyd and this is my woman Jean. This guy here is Notch."

"Hi, I'm Kate."

Kate had tried a lot of things but had finally settled on aircraft mechanics. She was rushing to Detroit to register for school the next day. Kate was small and square. She wore an expensive leather touring jacket and an open-faced helmet. The wind and bugs were no problem since she had a fairing, but she had gotten a bad sunburn and was daubing lotion on her face constantly.

She was talkative and quickly dominated the conversation with tales of her weekend ride up north where she had met a group of outlaw Harley riders in a bar. She had had a few drinks with them and they seemed nice.

I wondered if they were really outlaws. The few outlaws I knew never spoke to anyone other than a brother.

I had lunch with Kate. She was a vegetarian and she complained that her choices were always limited. I had an egg salad sandwich wrapped in clear plastic film and a cup of coffee in a white Styrofoam cup. When we were settled at a table I asked Kate why she rode such a tall bike.

"My old boyfriend said I should get a BMW because they are so reliable. I got a good deal on this one, so I bought it. I'm getting used to it. I still drop it a lot, but there is usually somebody around to help me pick it up."

All BMWs are tall motorcycles, so I asked, "Why don't you get a Honda or something like that?"

"Oh, no. I like owning a BMW and meeting all the BMW people. There are BMW riders everywhere I go. I just don't see many Hondas except for Gold Wings."

True. Honda sells a lot more motorcycles, but I had seen more BMWs on the road than anything else. Of course, that could be because I was on a BMW myself.

Still, would I ride a bike that was way too tall just because of brand loyalty? We're not talking Chevy people vs. Ford people.

We're talking falling down vs. staying upright. Luckily, I wasn't as short as Kate. It would have been a real problem.

The beginning, middle, and end of journeys are not intersections of latitude and longitude. This trip began when I learned to ride. When my father told me he rode an Indian across country in the late 1930s, a trip I now know only happened in his mind. When Jerry came to Hawaii leaving whatever past he had behind. When I sold my business and started shopping for a bike. And when I turned my back on the Atlantic and headed west.

The middle of a trip is not a simple matter of dividing by two. The middle of this trip happened in Mexican Water, Arizona, when I realized I was going to make it the whole way. When I stopped leaving and began returning.

Journeys end slowly and reluctantly. We think they should be clear and triumphant matters, like finishing the Boston Marathon. But worthwhile journeys are not races. There are no prizes at the end, not even a T-shirt.

The end of this journey started when I retraced my path to Haines Junction and back down the Frazer Valley. When I plotted and abandoned a fast northern route around Lake Michigan. When I began staying in motels so I could ride longer days and more direct routes. As thoughts of home occupied more and more of my mind.

It finally ended shortly after I got off the ferry, when the two-lane highway I was following unexpectedly became a smooth, clean, safe expressway. My mind was already home and I welcomed the speed and efficiency of the modern road, so the bike could catch up with me.

But the bike was used to country roads. Stopping at restaurants with lots of pickups in the parking lot. Slowing before passing a farm tractor with a wave of the hand. Laying over in tight turns as the road followed a creek to its source. It regretfully settled in at 65 mph, sorry that the long ride was over, its special skills no longer needed.

The journey ended when getting home became more important than the potential of a road with a single white line down the center. When I was finally willing to give up the wonderfully un-expected back roads of America to get there faster. To get there faster? Ah, it's over.

Postscript

I got home okay and slowly drifted back into suburban life.

With all the rain that summer, the lawn needed mowing every week. When my riding mower broke, I bought an almost-new 21-inch mulching mower at a garage sale. It took two hours to do the front and back yards, pushing the roaring beast back and forth in precisely overlapping parallel lines. Some days I went north to south. Other days I went east to west. When my neighbor offered to lend me his riding mower, I told him I enjoyed the exercise.

I was driven by the urge to get rid of things I didn't need or use.

I donated plastic bags full of clothes to Goodwill. I emptied two of the four drawers in my dresser. There were blank spaces in my closet where my suits and dress shirts used to hang. I kept one suit for weddings and funerals. I got rid of the last of my Navy uniforms. Miraculously, the jackets still fit, although snugly.

Every week, I carried a heavy box of paper to the curb for recycling. I recycled years of records, some stretching back to my college days. I had not looked at any of them since they had been put away.

I gave away useless things hidden in the basement, in closets, and in the backs of drawers. Old trophies and incentive awards from my corporate days. Odd items that we somehow got, but never used. Good intentions and false starts. Dumb purchases. And things I never got around to fixing.

I took boxes of books to the library for their book sale. I went over and over the bookshelves, forcing myself to take out books I knew I would never read or look at again. I still have too many books, but the collection is more focused now.

I sold my fishing equipment at a neighborhood garage sale. My neighbors bought all of it before the public had a chance. Fly-casting, spin-casting, and bait-casting equipment. Rods, reels, lures, tackle boxes, waders, my vest. Everything went except for the surfcasting equipment I gave to my brother in Hawaii.

When I was done, I still thought I had too much stuff, so I decided to get rid of something every day. That would eventually force me to deal with all the stuff I kept piece by piece. Some days are hard, others easy.

I turned off the radio in my car and drove in silence. We stopped watching TV, using it only for an occasional movie on the VCR. We stopped eating meat at home except when we entertained. When people asked what I did, I started saying I was retired. I stopped looking for business opportunities. When my old business associates learned I was no longer in the game, they stopped calling.

Our circle of friends expanded to include people in the motorcycle club, members of the Zen Center, and people in the photo history community. People pursuing their true interests or indulging their obsessions.

I had entered a year-long certificate program in photographic preservation. I enjoyed the craft, working with paper and metal and wood. I learned museum quality framing. I restored Margaret's and my mother's wedding portraits and they sit on our family altar.

I started looking at pictures again. Not just photographs, but paintings and drawings as well. I rediscovered light and form and texture.

I developed an interest in antique photographic processes. I learned to make tintypes by pouring liquid collodion on black metal plates, sensitizing the plates in a liquid silver bath, and exposing and developing the image while the collodion was still wet. Since the imaging material is white, the black backing produces a dim but recognizable image. Thousands of Civil War soldiers carried tintypes of their sweethearts and had lined up at photographer's tents for portraits they could send home.

I learned to make daguerreotypes by carefully polishing a silver plate, sensitizing the plate with iodine fumes, and exposing and developing the plate with mercury fumes. The first viable photographic process, daguerreotypes still produce magical silvery images that fade and reappear as the plate is tilted. I learned to wear black clothes when viewing daguerreotypes since the dark shades on a daguerreotype are reflected by the silver plate.

I rediscovered large-format photography when I had to make large negatives for non-silver contact-printing processes. I bought an old wooden 5x7 field camera and wandered around taking pictures. People came up to talk, remembering when they or their fathers had used cameras like mine.

I made platinum prints and cyanotypes from the large negatives. I made carbon prints using material I bought at the supermarket. Knox gelatin. Hydrogen peroxide. India ink.

I found people who had devoted their lives to mastering these processes. It was like meeting another motorcyclist on the road. We had a secret language. When the right words were spoken, they were eager to connect. And always ready to help.

The ride goes on.

About the Author

Notch Miyake is a third-generation Japanese-American born in Hawaii. He began riding motorcycles in high school. After dropping out of the University of Hawaii, he worked as a photographer in Waikiki. Then he got his act together, graduated from the University of Puget Sound, joined the Navy, served in Vietnam aboard ship and in Danang, got an MBA from Columbia University, worked part-way up the executive ladder at Xerox Corporation, and left to run his own business. After making this trip, he stopped working for a living. He is married and has two children.